BOYS AND SEX

Other books by Wardell B. Pomeroy, Ph.D.:

Girls and Sex
Your Child and Sex
Dr. Kinsey and the Institute for Sex Research
Taking a Sex History

BOYS AND SEX

THIRD·EDITION

by
Wardell B. Pomeroy, Ph.D.

Co-author of the Kinsey Report
and author of *Girls and Sex*

Delacorte Press

Delacorte Press and Laurel-Leaf Books
Published by
Dell Publishing
a division of
Bantam Doubleday Dell Publishing Group, Inc.
666 Fifth Avenue
New York, New York 10103

RL: 9.9

Library of Congress Cataloging in Publication Data

Pomeroy, Wardell Baxter
    Boys and sex / by Wardell B. Pomeroy.—3rd rev. ed.
        p. cm.
    Includes bibliographical references (p.).
    Summary: Discusses the physical, emotional, and ethical aspects
of sex including such topics as pre-adolescent sex play,
masturbation, homosexuality, dating and petting, intercourse and
its consequences, and other related topics.
    ISBN 0-385-30250-9 (hc) ISBN 0-440-20811-4 (pbk)
    1. Sex instruction for boys. 2. Sexual ethics—Juvenile literature.
[1. Sex instruction for boys. 2. Sexual ethics.]
    I. Title.
    HQ41.P614 1991
    306.7'0835'1—dc20   90-3140
                                                                   CIP
                                                                    AC

Manufactured in the United States of America

February 1991

10 9 8 7 6 5 4 3 2 1

BVG

*This book is fondly dedicated
to my three children,
David, John, and Lynne*

Contents

Preface to the Third Edition

Two decades have gone by since the first edition of *Boys and Sex*. In that relatively short time the turmoil of the sixties has given way to the kind of sexually free society that seemed to be the property of the Great Awakening at Woodstock in those days.

Today there is an unprecedented flow of images and words about every aspect of sex thrown at us from television, advertising, magazines, books, newspapers, and movies. Sometimes it seems that sex is no longer a private matter, but is simply inescapable. The new generation of teen-agers appears on the surface to be coping with it better than one might expect, but the rise of teen-age pregnancies, of AIDS and other sexually transmitted diseases, and of permissive behavior that would not have been permitted a generation ago tells us that the need for information is still there, despite the seeming sophistication of the present high school crowd.

In preparing this third edition of *Boys and Sex,* trying to make its language easier and up to date, attempting to update information as well and orient teen-agers and preteen-agers to a changed world, I've been struck over and over by how *much* things have changed in those two crowded decades. Advice that made sense twenty years ago doesn't seem to have much relevance to the present.

Yet there are a good many things that *don't* change. AIDS may be new, and I have dealt with that here, but the fundamental relationship of the sexes and the sexual development of boys (and girls) haven't really changed fundamentally. The most profound effect on them has been made by the women's movement, the gay liberation movement, and the greatly relaxed censorship of motion pictures and printed matter. True, there has been a backlash. The eight conservative Reagan years disclosed a yearning on the part of some older people to return to what seemed a more comfortable and less complicated past. But the tide continues to roll, and no one can tell where it will end—or whether it will be reversed.

In light of all these factors, there seemed to be a clear necessity to produce a third edition, and the result is to be found in the following pages. In doing so, I've enjoyed once more my collaborator of the past twenty years, John Tebbel, who has been my right hand from the beginning in all my books.

Most of the material in this book has been distilled from my own professional experience, which would not have been possible without the late Dr. Alfred C. Kinsey and the Institute for Sex Research at Indiana University, with which I was associated for two decades. I'm most grateful to them both for the unique opportunity they gave me to learn about the sexual behavior of the human male and female in the United States.

BOYS AND SEX

An Introduction for Boys and Their Parents

There is no universal activity engaged in by human beings that causes so much unhappiness, disappointment, and misery as what happens in people's sex lives. What should be simple and beautiful, one of the great joys of our time on earth, too often becomes difficult and ugly.

I learned this for the first time a half century ago when I helped to compile what came to be known as the Kinsey Reports. During the research that produced these landmark books, I took the sexual histories of more than eight thousand different people (plus two thousand others in later years), ranging from young children to individuals over ninety. They came from every part of the United States and from every social and economic level; far too often I found that their sex lives had been a record of unhappiness, disappointment, even misery.

It would be comforting to think that we've come a long way since then. After all, we are much more frank about sex than we were fifty years ago. Movies, television, and the other media talk about it and display it in ways that would have been unthinkable when I began working in this field. But the public's greater or lesser acceptance of sexuality isn't matched by people's private behavior. As any therapist will tell you, the same old problems persist, and so do the same old factors that cause them. In an overwhelming number of cases, the two major factors are misinformation and simple ignorance. The puritanical past refuses to go away. We still have some of the same myths, fears, and inhibitions about sex that our grandparents and their parents suffered from.

This may be the best place to tell you how *I* feel about sex. I believe that we're all sexual beings and that sex is pleasurable. It happens to us in one form or another all our lives. Those who still think that it's something boys and girls can just postpone until they're in their twenties don't understand human sexuality. But it's also true, I think, that we live in a real world where whatever we do has consequences, and we have to learn to live in a society whose laws and established customs are basically antisexual. Penalties are waiting for those who think they can do whatever they please, and lives can be ruined by them.

I advocate a simple code of sexual behavior. Don't do anything that will harm other people, especially a sex partner. Don't force sex on people who reject it for one reason or another; any sex that's worth having has to be mutually desired. And finally, accept your own sexuality as a fact of life, something to be nurtured and used for your own and others' enjoyment. If your religious faith teaches otherwise, you'll have to learn how to make decisions about it that will satisfy your conscience. Fear and guilt are deadly enemies of a happy, healthy sex life.

The real world applies its own penalties to those who think that because we're able to talk about sex so freely these days, and see it exhibited everywhere we look, we can indulge ourselves freely. Teen-age mothers, for instance, face a life that is extremely difficult and costly. Those who take sex wherever they can get it simply because it's available run the deadly risk of AIDS, the worst killer since the days before syphilis was conquered by penicillin. But syphilis hasn't gone away; resistant strains have developed and it remains a menace, along with less potentially dangerous venereal diseases such as herpes. Herpes won't kill you, but it can make your life a misery, and there is no known cure.

These are the chief dangers to a happy sex life. In another chapter I'll tell you more specifically how to deal with them. They are consequences that can be avoided simply by knowledge and common sense.

Otherwise, everyone is entitled to a rewarding sex life, according to his or her own desires, and we have learned in this century that having sex is a joyful and enriching experience at any age. It begins when we're very young, and it doesn't need to stop even when we're very old.

To look at our society today, it seems sometimes that sex is the major part of living and that everyone devotes a great deal of time to it. The truth is that it's a vital part of life but it's far from being the whole thing, and people vary greatly in how much of it they need. Once we understand that, it's easier to be more comfortable with whatever kind of sex life we work out for ourselves. We just have to keep remembering that not everyone is the same, and we need to respect other people's feelings about it.

We also need to be careful about blaming sex for everything that goes wrong in our lives. Sex certainly plays an important part in the high divorce rate and in the fact that larger numbers of people aren't getting married at all, as well as in the ordinary everyday problems of living together. But there are a good many other factors involved in all these troubles—the clash of careers, finances, and other circumstances.

Where sex is the problem, very often it occurs either because people don't have the information available to them or because they can't relate what they think they know to their own lives. We watch sex on movies or television, and read about it in books and magazines, but not necessarily to understand *why* it's happening, or what it means to your own life. Information, *correct* information, is essential, and that's what I've tried to provide in this book, and it's why I wrote it. I can't count the times I've heard patients say to me, when I was a practicing sex therapist, "If only I'd been given more information about these things when I was young, or if only I'd had a more open attitude about sex, then maybe I wouldn't have made such a mess of my life."

The trouble begins at home. Parents have always found it hard to talk about sex with their children, much less in an informed and intelligent manner. They still find it difficult or impossible even with today's freedom. Parents may say, as so many do, that the home, not the school, is the place for sex education, but a very small percentage of people ever get that kind of education. Fortunately the schools have begun to take on the responsibility in a responsible way. However, sex education has spread unevenly across the country, against continuing opposition, and good programs are still balanced by bad or inadequate ones.

In taking the place of parent and school here, in an effort to help both, I'm going to be as forthright, direct, and honest as possible about the sex life of boys. (I've written another book for girls.) In the process, I intend to avoid moral judgments. Teaching morality is the province of parents and religious institutions. The boys themselves are likely to make their own codes of conduct. My object is simply to provide accurate information.

I hope parents will accept the idea that I'm being

neither permissive nor strict. I'm not urging boys to engage in sexual behavior of any kind. The great majority of them, with only an insignificant percentage of exceptions, have already engaged and are engaging in some kind of sexual behavior, and once started, they aren't likely to stop.

Having accepted this reality, we can move on to the next question—how to help boys understand what they're doing, and how to deal with any problems that may arise from it? When parents have tried to do this, they not only have failed to solve the problems in most cases but often have become part of the problem themselves. Simply telling children to stop sexual activity, which fills them with guilt and fear in the process or makes them feel ridiculous, is the kind of approach that is certain to fail. Many parents understand this now, but usually they don't know of any better approach. It's my hope that this book will help parents reach out to their sons on the subject of sex with more understanding and human warmth.

I intend to cover every kind of sexual behavior, beginning with preadolescent sex play, then masturbation, sexual activity with girls, the whole business of "dating," now called simply "going out," intercourse and its consequences, and other aspects of sex. I hope that from reading about all this, boys will be able to construct a framework that will help them to understand and deal with their sexuality, no matter what form it takes.

Boys (and girls, too) are going to get sex education of some kind from their earliest days, whether parents like it or not. They keep learning in one way or another as long as they're at home, regardless of whether the word "sex" is even mentioned. When an embarrassed father covers up his genitals hastily if he happens to be in the presence of a child who is only two weeks old, he's providing that child with sex education. When he embraces his wife warmly in front of the child, expressing his own sexual feelings, that's educational, too. Children absorb knowledge from what they see and hear.

We need to make a distinction here, I think—between the feeling that sex is private and the feeling that it's shameful. Obviously parents shouldn't engage in intercourse, or even heavy breathing contact with lips and hands before their children. Sex *is* a private matter. But at the same time, if parents make sex seem shameful, even by implication, they give their children the kind of sex education that may at some later time make it hard for them to make a satisfying sexual adjustment.

Parents today complain that they have a difficult time communicating with their teen-agers, but that's always been the case. A good argument could be made that it's worse today, but what hasn't changed is the fact that parents have always been able to give information to a child, of any age, about almost every aspect of life—except sex. They tell their children what they should eat, what to wear, what they should do or not do at home, how to preserve their health. But when it comes to sex, a great gulf opens between them.

Silence on the subject is sex education, too. If a boy never hears anything about sex from his parents, if any evidence of it in his parents' lives is carefully concealed, he may well feel that the reason for all this secrecy is that sex is something dirty and secret. This impression is often reinforced from the beginning. The first words most children hear from their parents about sex is, "Take your hands away from there!" Later natural curiosity about sex comes to the surface, but too often questions are turned away with embarrassment or with "You're too young to know about such things."

A parent who really wants to help can take advantage of a thousand opportunities to do so and provide information without any pretense. It can be done without giving the subject any more emphasis than it requires. Nor does the parent need to go out of his or her way to do it. There's enough in the news these days to provide any number of openings—celebrity adulteries, rape, child molesting, the spread of AIDS, the abortion controversy, censorship battles, not to mention the themes of many television and movie plots. Children often ask questions about these things and equally often are turned away with evasions.

Other events offer less obvious opportunities. Curfews are imposed, let's say, in a town or neighborhood where a rapist is known to be operating. A movie, or a book, or a rock lyric is censored, or someone argues that these should be, and that provides a chance to answer a young person's "Why?" whether or not the parent agrees. Even such an innocent subject as nutrition can provide an opening, especially in the case of early adolescents. It opens up the whole subject of pubertal changes and what they mean.

One cautionary note: Parents should remember, always, that the *way* they convey sex information is all-important; otherwise, they will hear that old battle cry "Don't preach to me." Parents need to get off their moral soapboxes and speak casually about sex, as they would about anything else, simply as part of everyday life. Comparisons—"When I was your age" or "Boys didn't do things like that when I was growing up"—are fatal.

Boys and parents alike need to remember that there is the widest possible variation among people in their attitudes toward sex. Everyone knows the official attitude, which is expressed in codes and laws. These regulations forbid any kind of sexual activity outside marriage, and there are some things people do every day without thinking that are accepted grudgingly, if at all, by legal and religious codes. "Normal" is the key word here. Those who hold to the official attitude are intolerant of any kind of sexual behavior they believe isn't "normal." They measure normality by what *they* do or think they should do. Extremists among them would like to forbid public or even scientific discussion of sex.

Other people aren't as rigid. They admit sex exists, but their argument is that young people ought to learn self-control and discipline. "Just say no" to sex, they advise, as they would with drugs. They want adolescents to follow the same conventional moral code they do, and while they sometimes go so far as to discuss sexual problems with their children, they aren't likely to yield very much.

The good news is that there appears to be a growing number of people who don't view sex in such absolute terms. They believe that what people do or don't do is not as important as the consequences of their actions on the people involved and those close to them. They realize that the values of their parents and grandparents are not the same as those of young people today, who live in a different world. Just the same, they think some kind of internal control by these same young people is necessary if they want to grow up healthy and happy at a time when it isn't so easy to be either.

The more liberal of these people think it ought to be possible for young people to have relatively complete sexual freedom. If their college-age daughter brings a male friend home from school for the weekend and expects to sleep with him in her old room, they swallow their memories and don't object. They understand that society has changed in some fundamental ways, but they don't think there has been a sexual revolution, only a gradual process of change in which some behavior is generally acceptable that was considered absolutely forbidden by the previous generation. People live together these days without getting married. Sexual activity may begin earlier than it did fifty years ago. Things can be talked about that were never mentioned then.

The healthiest attitude about sex is to regard it as

fun, and the more of it a person has, the better off he'll be, psychologically and physically. Therefore premarital intercourse is not in itself a bad thing if the consequences are kept firmly in mind and dealt with honestly. Such people ought to be well informed and well adjusted.

At the farthest end of this viewpoint are those "sexual anarchists" who attack chastity, virginity, and monogamy, who advocate suppressing all taboos and eliminating all ideas of immorality or shame. The only restriction they would impose is to require that people not injure or do violence to others. As you've already read, I stand at neither extreme and believe, in essence, that we have to learn to live realistic lives in a realistic society.

Social changes take place in spite of contrary and strongly held beliefs. No one condemns marriage as an institution, for example, but we have to understand that in our society today, it isn't necessarily good for everyone. Most people still get married, as they always have, but more than one out of four of these marriages ends in divorce; this figure rises and falls according to changing social conditions. It's worth remembering that three out of four couples choose to *stay* married, even though divorce is possible.

We are living now in an era when nearly half the working force is made up of women, and at the same time the number of single-parent families has increased dramatically. Children are often the victims of such social changes, and what they do sexually may be colored by them. There are also growing numbers of young people who prefer living alone, and that creates a whole new area of sexual and social problems.

Marriage is no longer the most important consideration. What is important is what happens in the relationship between two people and how they handle their sexual lives. That's why I believe the behavior and attitudes we develop toward sex while we're growing up can make a critical difference in the ability to work out satisfactory sexual adjustments in living with another person. It doesn't take a genius to figure out that if people have inhibited, restrained, and guilt-ridden attitudes about sex, they aren't likely to make those adjustments.

What people do sexually is not nearly so important as how they *feel* about what they're doing, and so the specific sex information given to children is not nearly so important as the attitudes that accompany it. And what are those attitudes? Simple, old-fashioned things like self-respect, responsibility, and openness, leading to a sense of what a lifetime pleasure sex can and should be.

That's why it's important that boys, and girls as well, learn what they need to know about sex as they are growing up. The information should be given with an attitude that inspires reassurance and acceptance of themselves and the world. If all this is done, these people are not likely to be upset later on in their lives by anything that happens to them sexually. If they grow up in ignorance about sex, except for what they can pick up in the street, they will eventually find themselves in an adolescent world, and later in an adult world, both of which are confusing and frightening and are worlds they don't understand.

Sex education isn't a package of knowledge, a large dose of information to be given once when the parent thinks it's needed. It's like any other kind of education: It has to be repeated before it can be retained.

That's why I'm addressing this foreword, and the book itself, to both boys *and* their parents. For boys approaching or entering adolescence, I hope it will be a guide to what's happening, or about to happen, to them. I hope it will dispel any guilt or fear about sexual behavior they may have, and will help them toward a well-adjusted sexual life as adults. For parents, I hope the book will give them information they can provide to younger children in whatever way they think best—a means of sexual guidance that combines information with reasonable attitudes rooted in reality.

Some parents reading this introduction may still be doubtful. If so, I urge them to review their own sex lives from the beginning when they think about how they're going to give their children sex education. Have they lived lives so perfect and satisfactory, so free of guilt and fear, that they've never had any problems with sex? Has sex never affected the quality of their lives? Then they should ask themselves whether they want something better for their sons and daughters than what was given to them when they were young. I hope the materials for that "something better" will be found in the pages that follow.

CHAPTER · 1

A Boy's Sex Life

Even to talk about "a boy's sex life" shows how far we've come in a few years. Your parents and grandparents weren't supposed to *have* sex lives, or if they did, it wasn't a subject that anyone cared to discuss unless a boy (or a girl) was in sexual trouble of some kind. Boys talked about sex a lot among themselves, and so did girls to a lesser extent and in milder terms, but now there is virtually nothing that boys and girls don't discuss *together* when it comes to sexual matters. They do it as casually as they would talk about anything else. Television and the movies, along with rock lyrics, have been the great educators.

Books for young people have changed radically with the times. Judy Blume, whose books for teenagers are immensely successful, talks freely about sex and its problems in the language of her audience. These books, with their frank talk about masturbation, intercourse, and homosexuality, could not have been circulated fifty years ago.

Because of the greater freedom we enjoy today, both boys and girls sometimes think they know a great deal more about sex than they actually do. Just because the words and the images are so free doesn't mean they are necessarily correct. Freedom, in fact, hasn't solved everyone's sexual problems, by any means, and it doesn't mean that a sexual revolution has really occurred, as we so often read or hear. Actually what has happened is a growing and speeded-up acceptance of sexuality by the general public, which doesn't always understand what it knows.

Acceptance shouldn't be confused with changed behavior. In spite of everything, sexual behavior is still a controversial subject, and all of us are affected by the controversies. Millions of people—young as well as older people—have very strong religious beliefs about sex. Others may not be particularly religious but nevertheless have firm ideas about what is right and wrong sexually—and that applies to children as well as to parents.

You will have your own attitudes about sex, just as all your friends and your parents and your other relatives do. What you believe may have been learned partly from parents or friends, or partly from other sources. For whatever reason, differences of opinion and belief exist; people don't think exactly alike about anything. What *is* important is that we must learn to live with people whose feelings and beliefs about sex may not be like our own.

So in talking about a boy's sex life, let's begin with a fundamental fact with which, in theory at least, everyone can agree, namely, that sex is or ought to be one of the most pleasurable activities available to human beings. It should be one of the happiest parts of our lives, from our earliest days until we're old. You can measure how free *you* are from fear and guilt by how much you agree with this fact.

That doesn't mean fear and guilt are unreasonable. Fear of pregnancy is real enough for both boys and girls. Fear of responsibility for it certainly affects both sexes. Fear of syphilis and gonorrhea may not be what it was, but we now have a greater fear to contend with —AIDS. Not to mention herpes and chlamydia.

Even when there's no overt sex involved, and so no fear of the consequences above, there is the fear of being put down by a girl, of being laughed at, and that is a very real fear for many boys. And when sexual behavior comes into conflict with religious beliefs, both fear *and* guilt are likely to be the result.

Leaving all these things aside, however, sex in all its forms is a normal, natural part of being human. What happens in a sexual act produces a pleasure beyond any of the other responses we make to the world we live in. It may have been designed to insure the perpetuation of the species, but it is also a universal enjoyment found in every kind of society everywhere in the world.

But we aren't free to enjoy sex in any way we like,

because we live in a society where nobody is completely free to do what he pleases. If we were, the result would be anarchy. This means an individual's sex life shouldn't get him or other people into trouble. Sex may not be shameful, but it *is* private. It's also regulated by every religion, and if you intend to live within the beliefs of your faith, whatever it is, you'll have to respect its regulations.

But leaving aside these and other restrictions, I intend to talk about sex here in a free and natural way, as though it were the happy, enjoyable thing it should be. We'll discuss the limitations later.

In the next chapter I'll discuss the simple physical facts of sex. They are easily understood, but their simplicity is misleading. What the human male does in a sex act may be physically simple, but nothing else he does is capable of having such important and varied consequences, so it's only sensible to be concerned about it. In adolescence boys are usually more concerned about sex than they've ever been before or may ever be again, because suddenly it has become one of the most important facts of their lives as they approach their sexual peak in their late teens.

So it's important to understand your sex life. With understanding, you'll be less likely to be upset about adolescent sex problems; later it will be easier for you to adjust to the adult world. For instance, if a girl rejects you, it's good to know some of the reasons so your relationship with another girl won't be affected. If you know about sex, it will also help you to get along better with adults. You have to live with *them,* too, and it's easier to live as friends than as enemies. If you understand your sex life, you'll understand better why parents and teachers behave the way they sometimes do in your relationships with them.

Knowledge of sex also teaches us something about the uses of power, a favorite subject in American life these days. Anyone who's ever been in love knows that when you're deeply involved with another person, the one who loves the most possesses the power to hurt the other, and on the flip side, the one who loves less or is not in love at all can hurt the other, too. People do have the capacity to hurt each other, and they often use that power. But it's also useful to realize that people can hurt *themselves.* If your best friend challenges you to jump into a pool with your clothes on and you refuse, he may call you a coward or a nerd, but you probably won't be too upset. He's your friend. But if he falls into the water accidentally and you refuse to try to rescue him if he needs it, he can call you "coward" if he survives, and this time you'll be hurt. The word is the same in both cases, but the effect is different.

In the first instance, no doubt you'd say to yourself, "Oh yeah, well, I don't see him jumping in so he's just as big a coward as I am. Anyway, it isn't being a coward if you don't want to jump in a pool with your clothes on." But in the second case, you might say, "I must be no good if I didn't even try to rescue my friend," or, in another kind of reaction, "He doesn't have a right to say such a terrible thing to me," which puts your friend in the wrong. In other words, it's your own thoughts about a situation that can hurt you, not what the other person says.

You don't have to be accepted or loved by other people for everything you do—and anyway, that would be impossible. There are some people we'd like to have love us, or at least approve of us. But they may have limitations of their own, and can't really love anyone. Or maybe they have irrational reasons for not liking other people, including you—the color of your eyes, the way you comb your hair, how you speak, or some trivial thing you may have said at the first meeting. People reject each other for all kinds of reasons.

Boys and girls who are too concerned about being loved will soon begin to worry about how *much* people love them, and how *long* they're going to keep on doing it. But they don't realize that if they were constantly loved, they would also have to be constantly lovable, and for most of us that would be impossible. Even if it were possible to win the approval of everyone you want to love you or approve of you, it would take all your time and energy to do it, and you'd find yourself living for what others thought of you instead of pursuing your own goals. It's sad but true that the more people think they need to be loved, the less others are likely to give it to them. People tend to think the need for love is a sign of weakness, and they are irritated by people who are constantly trying to win it.

It's also possible that being loved intensely may not be as good as it seems on the surface. The other person will almost certainly make great demands on your time and energy. Intense loving is a creative, absorbing act.

There's a difference between "needing" and "wanting" love. Boys and girls who have a great "need" for love and approval may really be trying to compensate for their feelings of worthlessness. In effect, they're saying: "I must be loved because I am a worthless, incompetent individual who cannot possibly get along in the world by fending for myself, so I *need* to be helped and cared for by others." But "wanting" love is a different thing. Nearly everyone *wants* love because that is the most important way human beings connect with each other. It's perfectly normal.

If you think, after reading this, that your need for love is excessive, in the way I've described, there are four things you can do. First, ask yourself what *you* want to do in life, rather than what other people want you to do. Second, you should be willing to take risks and commit yourself and not be afraid of making mistakes, to get what you want out of life. Third, focus on loving rather than on being loved. And finally, above everything else, stop confusing being loved with your feelings about your own personal worth.

Now, keeping those four points in mind, we come down to what I want this book to do. I want to give boys essential knowledge about sex so they can feel relaxed about it, even though what I say may not solve their particular problems. After all, this is not an advice book. It won't tell you what kind of sex you should have or how often you should have it, but it *will* tell you what's happening to you when you do it, whatever it is, and it will tell you something of how you may feel about it.

Everybody has sex of some kind, but what people do is as individual as they are. Everyone is different, and there are as many varieties of sexual behavior as there are people. Even a word like "adolescence," a blanket word covering the maturing that takes place in teen-agers, doesn't describe something that has a definite beginning and a definite end. It doesn't begin and end at the same time for everyone. Usually, for boys, it starts at about twelve to fourteen, when they begin to notice physical changes in themselves—more hair around the penis and under the arms, longer and thicker than the down that was there before. One day, at the climax of masturbation, an adolescent boy will see seminal fluid spurting from his penis for the first time. That means he is now biologically capable of creating another life. He and his family will probably notice how tall he's getting, and how his voice is changing in pitch from higher to lower. When he dresses or undresses, he notices a certain tenderness around the nipples on his breasts—"breast knots," they're sometimes called—and they're sensitive to the touch.

These are the standard symptoms of puberty, of beginning adolescence. It may not happen until boys are sixteen or even seventeen. Others may start maturing as early as nine or ten. Most, however, begin when they are between twelve and fourteen and are ready to leave adolescence behind when they're seventeen or eighteen.

A boy reading this book undoubtedly knows something about sex, maybe a good deal about it, from his own experience, or maybe in rare cases from parents or from sex education classes in school. There may even be a few who will find this book an introduction to the whole subject. Still others may not be much interested in sex yet and may even find the subject boring. But most are interested in sex from their earliest years. No one knows why there's so much variation, but it's not important where you find yourself on the scale of experience and interest.

I'm talking in these pages to the average boy who has an average, healthy interest in sex. He's interested in where he's been sexually while he was growing up, and he's even more interested in where he's going as he becomes a teen-ager. He has the ordinary number of sex problems, which means he worries about some things and has guilt feelings about others. He's full of both information and misinformation, probably more of the latter, even though he belongs to a generation with access to more sexual knowledge than those that have gone before.

If you fit this description, relax and enjoy yourself and learn. This book is for you.

CHAPTER · 2

How the Machine Works

Think of your body as the most complicated computer ever devised. You can't use it properly, however, until you know how it works and in this case how it's programmed for sex.

Unfortunately, there are still two sets of programs, in spite of all the sexual freedom that prevails. One is the set of names used for sexual parts and actions that the doctor uses and are in the dictionary. The other is the polite pretense we continue to make that other names don't exist in conventional conversation, or in most newspapers, in spite of what we hear on the motion picture screen and the home video. That set used to be called "dirty words," and boys used to write them on walls and sidewalks, as some still do. It was a gesture of revolt against conventional society, as though the writer were saying, "I know these words and I know they offend people. I hope they offend you."

We're not nearly so offended any more. World War II marked the turning point, and since then there has been a steady acceptance of so-called four-letter words in movies, books, some magazines, and on the stage, though much less so on television and in newspapers. Some of these words have become a part of everyday speech.

I'm going to use the technical words here, not because I think the others are "dirty," but because the technical ones are the language of psychology, the profession I practice. In Chapter 10, ". . . I Forgot to Ask," I'll explain a few of these "dirty words," only because boys who use them often don't really know what they mean. There are many other ways of saying "penis," for example, and the numerous synonyms for "sexual intercourse" are heard around the world.

To begin, it's a fact that the penis is the central point of the male's body, as far as sex is concerned. It's a part any boy can be proud of, so graceful and beautiful in its construction that the greatest sculptors have reproduced it in marble and the finest artists of all ages in their paintings. The same thing, of course, can be said for the female body, including its sex organ, the vulva, with its small clitoris.

Penises come in all sizes. There's no truth to the belief that boys or men with large ones are any more sexually potent or powerful than those with small ones. Boys often worry about this, though. Some think they have unusually small penises because they're viewing them at an angle, from above, and the growth of pubic hair makes it seem shorter than it really is. It's also true that a long, limp penis will not gain as much length in erection as a shorter one, because of the circulation of the blood in the erectile tissue.

When a boy reaches adolescence, his penis will probably be of average size, which is six inches when erect. If it's below average then, it may grow later, but even if it doesn't, there will be no difference in the amount of sexual pleasure it can give, in spite of anything you've heard about big penises. Nor will it make any difference in how you perform sexually. "Average" means a point that is halfway along the range of penis sizes. Some may be smaller, some larger, but whatever its size, the penis will become erect when stimulated, either for nonsexual reasons or for specifically sexual ones.

Beneath the penis is a loose bag called the scrotum, which contains two testicles that are made from a complicated arrangement of tubes and cells. This is where the sperm cells are manufactured—the tiny organisms that contain the seeds of a new life when united with a female egg from the ovaries. Sperm can be seen only under the microscope. They're very active; they move by lashing their long tails. Their heads contain all the elements that make up our heredity—color of eyes and hair, height, mental and emotional characteristics—just as the egg carries the hereditary characteristics of the woman. United, sperm and egg make a new human being.

When a male is sexually stimulated, the first thing that occurs is erection of the penis. That's because blood flows down into its tissues, congests them, and makes the organ rigid and hard. Erection has been observed at all ages, in tiny infants and very old men— even before birth. In fact, many boy babies are *born* with erections. The penis, the scrotum, and the anus (where excrement comes from) are all very sensitive to sexual stimulation.

Erection can occur for other reasons, however. Healthy young males are capable of three or four erections a night, and those of all ages often find themselves waking up in the morning with an erection caused by sexual dreams. More rarely, it can also occur from lifting very heavy loads or by straining when moving the bowels. Boys who wear tight jeans have long since discovered that irritation from them can also cause erection. Swimmers learn, too, that it's possible to have one as a reaction to cold water.

Whatever the cause, when the stimulation reaches a certain point, sperm emerge from the testicles in a sticky substance called the seminal fluid. It looks globby, has a milky color, and spurts out through the opening of the penis.

But the penis has another function as well. A tube called the urethra runs up through it into the body and connects with the bladder, making it possible for males to urinate through it. Just below its connection with the bladder, the urethra is joined by another tube, like one river flowing into another. This tube comes around the bladder and connects with the testicles, so that a pathway is provided for the sperm to come out of the testicles, travel through the tube, enter the urethra, and flow on out the penis. When that happens, we call it an ejaculation—or a boy "comes," as we say.

The whole body is involved in this action. Respiration and heartbeat increase; a flush covers parts of the body. The climax of the ejaculation, what we call an orgasm, seems almost like a spasm of the whole body mechanism. After that, everything calms down quickly. Blood flows back out of the penis, which returns to normal size after being large and swollen. The whole body recovers quickly. If a male is young, as you are, he can be restimulated quickly, and the whole process can be repeated quite soon. But as boys grow older, the time it takes to do this slowly lengthens with age, and although men are never too old to have erection and orgasm if they are physically healthy, it is a longer process in old age.

I can sum up simply the physical action I've just described. It's the basis of male sex because it's the beginning of the process by which babies are made.

In this age of free sexual information, are there still boys who don't know how this works, how girls get pregnant? Unfortunately, there are millions of them, as the number of unnecessary pregnancies increase. Other things are involved, of course, in these unwanted pregnancies, but often it is simple ignorance. A boy may know that if he puts his penis into a girl's vagina and comes there, he is doing something that may result in pregnancy, but he may also have all sorts of wild ideas that make him feel the odds are on his side. But he won't think that if he knows how his sexual computer works.

This is how it actually operates. When a boy ejaculates into a girl's vagina without a condom, or if she is not using any kind of birth control device, the millions of sperm cells in his semen begin to lash their tails and move forward in the vagina. (I'll describe that organ later.) They swim into the narrow opening called the cervix near the end of the vagina. The cervix opens into the uterus (the womb). This is a pear-shaped organ that looks something like a very small cow's head, with the Fallopian tubes symbolizing the "horns." These tubes connect the uterus with the ovaries. The sperm continue to swim through the uterus into these "horns." There they may encounter an unfertilized egg cell coming from the ovaries. The eggs are made there and descend once a month down the Fallopian tubes.

If the sperm find an egg in the tube, they begin a fierce bombardment of it. Lashing their tails, they surround the ripe egg cell and try to penetrate it. This is when a pregnancy may occur, as a sperm manages to get through the egg wall and merges with it. Immediately the cell wall hardens and prevents any more sperm from getting in. The successful sperm cell then becomes a part of the egg's nucleus, while the others that failed to penetrate the egg die in a few hours. The period from the time the sperm are ejaculated until one of them reaches an egg cell (which does not always happen) may be as much as three hours or longer.

Joining of sperm and egg is called fertilization. This is the moment when the baby is conceived and its sex is determined. Sperm carrying Y chromosomes make boys; those carrying X chromosomes make girls. The sex of a child depends on which kind of sperm cell fertilizes the egg cell—in other words, it is pure chance.

Chance is involved in much of the whole process, as you can see. The sperm has to be in the Fallopian tube at the time the egg is traveling through it. The sperm must be vigorous, and the egg must be ripe. A woman produces only about four hundred ripe eggs in her entire lifetime, and there are only about twelve to twenty-four hours in every month when it is possible for a ripe egg to be fertilized.

Pretty good odds, you may be thinking. It sounds like an exciting sort of sexual Russian roulette. But read Chapter 8, "Consequences of the Real Thing," before you decide to take the chance. After that, I think you may want to recalculate the odds.

If an egg is not penetrated by a sperm in the Fallopian tube, it passes down through the uterus and is absorbed in the vagina. That's no problem. It's hardly visible to the naked eye. The whole process it just went through is called ovulation, and it happens only once a month, about halfway through the menstrual cycle. If fertilization has occurred, no more ripe eggs will be produced by the ovaries until after the baby is born. As for the fertilized egg, it moves out of the Fallopian tube into the uterus, nestles into the uterine wall, and the baby begins to grow there until it is ready to be born.

This is how your sexual computer works, and how your girl friend's works, too. These are the basic facts you need to know about the anatomy and physiology of sex. A great deal more has been written about the subject, enough to fill a large library, but what I've told you here are the important things. I'll be talking later about pregnancy as a consequence of sexual intercourse.

CHAPTER · 3

Learning About Sex

Your sex life, like everybody else's, probably began before you were born. Some researchers think it starts while the unborn child is still being carried by its mother. They have observed rhythmic masturbatory movements in the womb among male fetuses, but since girls don't have such unmistakable signs of sexual feeling, it's not so easy to determine when they first feel the sex impulse. There is no reason, however, to believe that it happens any later than it does for boys.

We've learned these things only recently. For a long time, doctors had a completely erroneous idea of how children developed sexually. It was believed by generations of physicians that during the first seven years children had sex feelings they knew nothing about and did nothing to excite or relieve what they were not conscious of. After that, it was said, came six or seven years when there was little, if any, sexual activity. Freud called this the period of latency. The onset of adolescence was supposed to mark the great change when the whole business of sex was presumed to break over a child like a summer thunderstorm.

Today we know there's no truth in these ideas. Many children make attempts to stimulate themselves sexually by masturbating as soon as they can coordinate the motion of their hands and arms, and even before that they may find other ways to do it.

Another old and equally false belief is that children don't have orgasm until they reach adolescence. We know now that both male and female babies as young as four to six months have orgasm. No ejaculation occurs in the boys simply because the semen has not yet developed in their glands, but the feeling is the same, and it can be just as pleasurable and exciting as it is later. What comes later is psychological stimulation. If you're feeling cheated because you haven't had an orgasm, don't worry. Not all boys have them before they're able to ejaculate; some do and some don't.

If you have an infant brother, you may have seen him lying on his stomach and pushing his penis against the bed or the floor with a thrusting motion. Does he know what he's doing? Not in the sense that he'll know later on, but already he's aware that stimulating his penis will produce a pleasurable sensation. Maybe you've also seen him asleep in his crib but rocking back and forth rhythmically on his hands and knees, sometimes so hard the crib bangs against the

wall. This is sometimes, but not always, another example of the powerful sexual impulse at work, impelling
him to imitate, unconsciously, the movements of intercourse.

At this stage of infancy, a baby is still not able to
coordinate his movements and put his hands on his
penis in order to stimulate it, but he learns how to do
that in time. However, a sizable percentage of boys
don't begin to masturbate until they are considerably
older, somewhere near the beginning of adolescence,
although it isn't unusual or a sign of abnormality if it
begins earlier.

Whenever stimulation begins, it's often carried
through to the point of orgasm. The difference is that
semen is not ejaculated until adolescence, and only
semen can impregnate a girl if you have intercourse
with her. When people talk about "coming," they
mean either ejaculation (something is "coming" out
of the penis), or else they mean orgasm, which is sexual climax, the sudden release of sexual tension.
That's what we mean when we talk about orgasm before puberty in boys. And it's sexual climax we're talking about when we say a girl "comes."

It doesn't take long to reach orgasm, and the time
varies with age. Two to three minutes is the average
time before adolescence. Later, in the chapter on masturbation, I'll talk about how this time can be considerably prolonged and why it may be a good thing to do
so. After adolescence begins, nearly all boys ejaculate
within ten minutes, but about a third come in less than
a minute. Of these fast workers, about half have sev-

eral orgasms in a row, the second coming in approximately another minute and the third two minutes or so later. Some boys have even more successive orgasms.

But no matter how long or short a time it takes, and whether the orgasms are few or many, it's nothing to worry about. These variations are simply one more example of the many differences among human beings. Girls experience the same kind of variations.

All these things—having sexual feelings, experiencing orgasm, masturbating—are a natural part of growing up. It's the same as learning what pain is like, or what girls are like, or what you can do and can't do in the society you live in, or how to play a sport. We grow up in a world full of all kinds of things. Not everyone experiences everything, but sex experiences are common to all.

You may have already discovered that something "sexy" is not necessary to arouse sexual feelings. In fact, the stimulation is sometimes completely nonsexual. For example, when a boy is very young, it's easy for him to have an erection, and it may arrive quickly, before he knows what's happening. When he gets older, it isn't as easy as it was before, and then the stimulation has to be more specific.

For a very young boy, erections can happen suddenly for reasons unrelated to sex. Excitement over almost anything can produce erection. Even being frightened can create a sexual response. Sometimes it can come from nothing more than the friction of tight jeans against the penis. Boys used to like to put their hands in their pockets, and naturally they touched the

penis from time to time, producing a quick erection—
your father called it "pocket pool." The coming of
tight jeans, however, changed that habit for most
boys, but the tightness in the crotch has made up for it.

Another common experience for a boy is to be
called on in class to read something or provide an
answer he isn't really prepared to do. The resulting
excitement and anxiety may generate an erection even
more noticeable in today's jeans than it used to be in
pants. It can be an embarrassing experience, but
there's nothing much he can do about it. If anybody
makes fun of him later, he can always reply that the
same thing could happen to the teaser. It's simply the
way boys are made.

Other nonsexual things may cause erection in a
young boy besides those I've just mentioned. It's a
long list. Being spanked sometimes does it. Various
kinds of motion may produce it—riding a bicycle, taking a fast elevator, flying in an airplane, traveling by
train or bus, even sitting in a car or driving fast in it.
Erections might come if you're merely lying in the
warm sand on the beach, or diving, or swimming.

Emotion can also cause erections, but they're not
necessarily sexual. Fear of something might do it, or
anxiety about taking a test, or seeing some authority
figure you might be afraid of even if there's no reason
to be, or watching a fire, playing in an exciting game,
being alone at night, or falling.

Of course, it's the specific situations causing erections that you're most likely to notice. Like seeing a
particular girl, or watching a good-looking one, or

simply thinking about a girl. These are common causes. Telling sexy jokes, or looking at an erotic picture, or seeing pictures of girls who may not even be in sexy poses can cause an erection. In these cases it's the imagination that supplies the stimulus. Boys can even get an erection from seeing their own bodies in the bathroom mirror or from seeing other boys' genitals.

Some less obvious sources of stimulation may lead to both erection and orgasm. Urinating is one, and so is being stimulated by the water in a shower or bathtub. Sometimes it happens when a boy rubs himself down with a towel, or feels the vibration of a vehicle, or slides down a railing, or climbs a tree. Daydreaming is a very common way to produce it, and so is reading a book. There are literally dozens, probably more, things that may stimulate a boy to orgasm, but by far the most common is self-masturbation.

Humans are curious. Babies start crawling about the floor, exploring the world. As soon as they can stand and walk, they continue their explorations. At some point this curiosity extends to other children, after they've satisfied themselves about their own bodies. Boys want to find out if other boys are like them, and they also want to know if girls are different.

Again, there's a great difference in age when such exploration begins. No two boys are exactly alike. At five, one out of ten will have had some sex play with other boys or with girls. In the next five years, more of them discover each other. By the time they are ten, more than a third will have had sex play, more than half of these with other boys and nearly half with girls.

Before adolescence, three-fourths have had sex play with either boys or girls, or both. Of course, this behavior varies with geographical, environmental, and economic factors.

Probably you began your own sexual exploration in much the same way that most boys do, and most girls too—that is, exposing your genitals in return for an examination of someone else's. This is so common that it's given a phrase to our language: "You show me yours, and I'll show you mine." Millions of small boys and girls have also "played doctor," making a game out of sexual exploration. With this kind of make-believe, children feel free to look at and examine each other as much as they like. Research shows that about two-thirds of boys either masturbate another person or are masturbated by another during their preadolescent sex play. Often each does it to the other.

Small boys often want to try intercourse with their girl playmates. They've learned enough about it from reading or watching, or from the conversation of older, more informed boys. About half the boys who have preadolescent sex play make the attempt. About a quarter of them manage to insert their penises at least partially into the girl's vagina, sometimes even all the way, and go through the motions of intercourse.

Sometime before puberty, about one out of ten boys gets the idea of putting another boy's penis into his mouth. Children naturally like what psychologists call "oral behavior." As infants, they try to put everything that interests them into their mouths, so it's not remarkable that during their sexual explorations it occurs to some of them that a penis might taste good. Or they just want to see what it's like. This may happen only once, or it may be repeated. These boys will learn later that this kind of activity is a punishable offense for adults in every state and is considered abnormal by much of society. But in growing up, it's simply another part of learning what the human body is all about.

"Society" to most boys at this stage means father and mother. In these days of greater acceptance of sexual behavior, it may seem that parents are less strict today than they used to be, and that may be true to some extent. But it depends a great deal on the education and lifestyle of the parents. There are still not many of them who would not pull a small child's hands away from penis or vulva if a boy or girl innocently puts them there. That's often the first sex education children get. It tells them that there must be something wrong with sexual feelings, that if you touch yourself and it feels good, you must be doing something wrong, something you may even be punished for. Most don't understand yet the difference between expressing your sexual feelings in public and in private.

I can only hope your parents are the kind who knew how to say "no" gently and gave you reasons. Permissiveness, however, can be as bad as denial. Adolescents, at the normal stage of being in rebellion against their parents, may be confused if the parents have always let them do just about what they liked sexually, and may even resent that they were given such freedom and not told how to handle it.

On the other hand, it's unfortunate that so many parents still punish children for the kind of preadolescent sex play I've been describing and discourage it with stern warnings if they think it's going on out of their sight.

If something like this is happening to you, try to understand that when your parents punish you for sexual activity, or forbid it completely, they're only repeating what their parents did to them. Most children do it anyway, of course, but they suffer from guilt feelings as they try to hide their activities. So it's not surprising that when they grow up, they treat their children the same way. It may not be fair, but it's the way people have lived for generations. Change comes slowly, but it comes, and boys who read this book may act differently when *they* become parents.

Of course, it would be ideal if boys and their parents (girls, too) could learn from each other—if parents could understand, for example, that sex play before adolescence is a natural part of growing up, and that most children do it. Such sexual activity is healthy and enjoyable in itself and is even worthwhile if it helps children accept sex naturally. There's just one reservation, though. While most preadolescent sex play is healthy, it can be wrong and even dangerous if it's used to take advantage of other children. As I said earlier, it's wrong to force sex on someone who doesn't want it. It's also wrong if children are introduced to behavior for which they're not yet emotionally ready.

But where do we draw the line? When does it stop

being clean and healthy and become harmful? It's a big question. Fortunately, the answer is not very complicated. Boys see it every day on the playground when a bully teases, hurts, or abuses a smaller boy. That's what happens when sex play is wrong, except that the bully may not necessarily be older or larger. If he imposes his sexual desires on another child against the child's wishes or personal beliefs, he's no better than the bully who abuses a weaker child. There can be long-range effects from this kind of treatment. Resentment and anger in the victim may influence his feelings about people, or about sex, in the future.

So the danger is clear. If a child has to be argued into sex play, or bullied into it, or does it because he wants to gain some other child's favor—that isn't healthy sex.

Differences in age can also turn a healthy act into an unhealthy one. If sex play is involved, it's better for the two children to be near the same age. If there's a wide difference in age, it's usually the older boy who is exploiting or seducing the younger one. That's the kind of thing parents worry about when they try to prevent their children from having any sex play at all. It's also a danger in a family where an older boy may try to play sex games with a younger sister—or vice versa.

Now that we have identified the dangers, the good news is that playing with girls sexually before adolescence and trying to understand how they are made and how they react increases the chances for a satisfactory sex life when a boy grows up. Don't expect your parents to take that attitude, however. They remember what their parents told *them,* and they still have vague fears about what might happen. I'm sure many boys reading this will already have had sex play with girls, and those who haven't reached adolescence are likely to indulge in sexual activity with girls in spite of anything their parents or I or anyone else may say about it. They are simply following in the footsteps of millions of boys before them, many of whom have been able to lead happier lives as adults because of their early contacts with girls. But they will just have to understand that most parents disapprove of such activity.

What does that mean? It means privacy if you want to do such things. Both adults and parents have private areas of their lives, and *should* have them. In fact, everybody needs *some* kind of privacy, and sexual privacy is the most important kind to have. Many parents want their children to believe that sexual acts carried out in private must be "dirty." They want to know what you're doing behind the bedroom door. Small children learn quickly that if they follow their natural instincts and masturbate on the front lawn or in front of adults, they'll be punished, but if they do it in private and don't get caught, they can satisfy themselves. They have learned that sex is a private matter.

Whatever kind of sexual act a boy wants to do, he should do it with someone he knows. Now that child molesting has become a national scandal, even though it has always existed, mostly unreported, parents are more worried than they've ever been that their boy or girl may encounter an older man hanging around the school playground, or the candy store, or cruising along in a car. These are very real dangers, and parents are properly concerned about sexual bullies and exploiters. Too often, as the newspapers so frequently tell us, these men turn out to be kidnappers and murderers.

It's natural for parents to have these fears, and they are far from being unjustified, but at the same time another danger arises if small children are forbidden over and over to speak to any adult on the street, or if they are taught to be hostile and suspicious toward any adult who speaks to them, anywhere or anytime. If it's carried too far, the result may be a lifelong difficulty in dealing with other people. Boys need to understand that molesters, exploiters, and even more dangerous people are out there, and must be avoided, but the percentage of adult strangers they see in a day who belong in that class is so tiny as to be almost nonexistent.

In other words, there's a big difference between the man who kids you gently in the candy store and the one who stands outside and offers you something if you'll get into his car. To put them both in the same category, along with any other strange adult, is to lay the groundwork for a future problem. It isn't easy to erase suspicion and fear when it's firmly implanted in a young child's mind. And since, in this case, these feelings are connected with sex, it's easy to see how sex and adults can become something to be feared. This is true for boys, but even more so for girls.

The best policy is simple. Just be careful about sexual bullies, adult or your own age. There's usually something more to such a relationship than fun and games. As I've said, you're much better off playing such games with boys and girls your own age whom you know. In later life, you probably won't often have sex with strangers whom you've just met. Perhaps never. It's not a good idea then, and it isn't now.

In fact, sex among preadolescents usually involves children who *do* know each other well and play together. As I observed earlier, most boys play such sex games as mutual examination and manipulation well before puberty. Their own instincts lead them to these experiments. But there always seems to be a shyness and hesitation about doing such things with a new child in the neighborhood or a visitor. In childhood, as in later life, sex is usually most rewarding when it happens with someone you know well. All adults need to develop feelings of friendship and affection for their own well-being, and the time to develop these feelings is during the growing up process, when a child learns about living with other people.

There *are* real problems connected with preadolescent sex play, but they're not what many people think they are. Most adolescents have learned by that time what one of the worst problems is—being caught by an adult. A child caught in the middle of a sex experience and made to feel guilty and afraid is likely to begin feeling that sex is a dirty thing, something to be conducted secretly in a dark corner if at all. That can mean plenty of trouble in later life.

Another problem is the boy who has been labeled "bad." Maybe he's had some sex play with a child in the neighborhood who has gone home and told his mother, who then has forbidden her child to play with him again. When the boy's parents discover this and learn the reason for it, often from the parents of the offended child, punishment usually follows. But then the word may get around among other neighborhood parents, especially if the original discovery is repeated. But even if it isn't, once the story is known in the neighborhood, the offender is viewed with suspicion by all parents. And so a "bad boy," who has done nothing other children aren't doing, is started on a path leading to later trouble.

Finally, just remember that sex isn't something all by itself in your life, something isolated and secret. It's an essential and important part of the life of every human being, but it must be private to avoid collision with the rights of other people. It's worth remembering, too, that sex and affection for other people go together in good relationships. Sex is better and more fun if affection is involved than if it is practiced by itself for no better reason than because it's there.

Whatever form preadolescent sex play takes, the only real harm that can come from it, everything else being equal, is the feeling of guilt that may result. That can be more damaging than any sexual act. Some of the boys reading this book have just about reached adolescence, and if they've come that far without acquiring a load of guilt about what they've done sexually, they're lucky. If they *do* carry a guilt load, they should try to dump it as soon as possible. When they read this chapter, they'll see that whatever they've done has also been done by millions of other growing boys. No one needs to feel guilty or ashamed about these healthy and normal activities. Once that's understood, a boy is better prepared to deal with the much more difficult problems of adolescence itself.

CHAPTER · 4

Sex for Yourself

Not many people today would argue about whether boys have sex lives—or girls, either. This used to be the case, however. What should always have been obvious is accepted now. Every boy *does* have a sex life, and the only question is, what kind does he have?

Masturbation is by far the most common way a boy can express himself sexually, and it's common to boys all over the world. Nearly all human males masturbate. The few who don't got started in some other kind of sexual activity, such as intercourse, so early in life that they found no reason to masturbate. Other outlets may include fondling; actual intercourse with a girl, which happens only with a minority of boys; and homosexuality, or sexual activity between members of the same sex. Of these, the most common is fondling, which includes kissing and touching to some degree; most boys have done this by the time they reach adolescence.

We'll be talking about all these activities later, and about other outlets too, but let's begin with that most common form of sex, masturbation.

It's as old as human life itself, and as I've said, it's practiced in every country. Yet nearly every religion has had, or still has, some kind of prohibition against it. From a medical standpoint, it's hard to realize that even into this century, there were doctors who believed that masturbation "weakened" boys or caused various diseases in them, or produced insanity if "practiced to excess."

No one knows how many boys in the nineteenth century were taken to their doctors by parents, and heard the physician tell them: "I can tell you masturbate. Your pale face and glazed eyes and sweating palms and general ill health give you away." That was exactly what the poor boy feared, because he had been warned about all those things. Often the fear and guilt generated by the doctor's branding of him as a masturbator, and rousing his fears of inevitable insanity, were enough to produce all the symptoms the doctor thought he saw.

No reputable doctor believes such nonsense today, yet the weight of tradition and social pressure hasn't been greatly improved in spite of the far different climate we live in. True, masturbation is freely discussed in books for young people, and it's even occasionally depicted on the screen, sometimes in nonpornographic films. It's no longer in the closet, "the hidden vice," as it was once called.

But in everyday practice, as the records of sex therapists show, there are still a great many parents who think masturbation is wrong and unhealthy. They don't take extreme measures to stop it as they once did, but they make a child feel guilty or "dirty" if they catch him (or her) doing it. The first time many children learn about society's attitude toward masturbation is when a parent snatches the child's hand away from the genitals when he touches them in public. Instead of reassuring the child that what he's doing is okay but it must only be done in private, the parent offers a direct lesson: Self-stimulation is wrong.

A great deal can be said, however, for masturbation as a positive sexual experience. It can play a satisfying role in everyone's sex life from childhood until the last days. To begin with, it's a pleasurable and exciting experience, and it produces feelings that have been enjoyed by people universally from the beginning of human history. It's also easy to do and requires no special time or place, only privacy. Anyone can do it, and it's the most easily learned of all sexual activities—usually the one that's learned first.

Masturbation has a lot of other benefits, too. It releases tensions, and consequently it's valuable in many ways that affect both physical and mental health. Later I'll discuss some of the particular tension-releasing values that it possesses.

One of the best things it does is to provide a full outlet for fantasy and daydreaming, both so characteristic of adolescents. Masturbation is usually accompanied by fantasy, and it provides an outlet for all kinds of sexual activities a boy might never perform in reality.

Masturbation enriches an individual's sex life by offering variety, and it harms no one, since it is a strictly solitary activity, a private matter. Nor is it against the law, as long as it's done in privacy. Only a very young child masturbates in public before he learns about privacy, but if he's old enough to know the difference and does it anyway, with full understanding of what he's doing, then a personality problem exists that will probably require professional help.

Religions in general forbid masturbation, as I've said, but some Protestant sects don't condemn it morally. Other faiths may not specifically condemn it, but on the other hand, no religion encourages it. Yet masturbation is really a benign sexual activity. There's no danger from venereal disease, or AIDS (obviously), because there's no exposure to infection or blood. I will talk more about AIDS later. No physical harm can come from it, in spite of the old beliefs, no matter how frequently it's done, although that fact wasn't generally understood until a comparatively short time ago. Moreover, it's socially acceptable in some groups, and it's available when no one else is present.

These are all positive values of masturbation. But since nothing is perfect, there are also a few things about this most common of practices that ought to be considered. Boys who masturbate a great deal may miss the opportunity for other sexual experiences that aren't solitary. They may fail to learn about being intimate with other people, and that is one of the most important things in life.

At some levels of society, in spite of greater acceptance today, it's still taboo to masturbate, and if a boy lives in that kind of family, he will have more reason to resist feelings of guilt that parents or others may try to impose on him if they catch him masturbating. Another prime source of guilt is any religion that condemns the practice, and boys who are brought up in a strict faith are likely to experience a real conflict. This may make masturbation a less satisfying experience than it would otherwise be. Boys who fear being discovered by their parents also struggle with guilt conflicts, and that is not a healthy state of mind.

There are two more drawbacks that ought to be mentioned. If solitary masturbation continues to be the only form of sexual outlet an individual has as he grows older, it will be harder for him to function in an adult society. And if it is practiced without orgasm as the end result, it can be physically and emotionally frustrating. But that's rare. Most boys ejaculate when they masturbate.

Leaving all these ifs and ands aside, it's safe to assume that if a boy is approaching adolescence, or is already in it, he is masturbating with some degree of regularity, and probably has been for some time. Probably, too, he thinks everyone else does it the same way he does, but actually there's a great deal of variation. The most common way, practiced by most boys, is to make a fist and hold the penis in it, and then to jerk up and down with a vigorous stroking movement. As the boy becomes more tense and aroused, and a buildup of sexual pressure and excitement occurs, the stroke becomes faster and faster until orgasm results.

Since the most sensitive part of the penis is at the tip, some boys employ a less vigorous method, using their fingers to stroke the head, increasing the motion until it is very rapid and orgasm occurs. A minority of boys, probably no more than 5 to 10 percent, lie on their bellies and use a pushing motion to rub the penis against the bed or a pillow, in a movement like intercourse itself. Younger boys use this method more often.

Some boys use all these methods, doing it one way, then another way next time, or employing all three methods in the same session. Usually, though, boys tend to fix on one method and don't often depart from it—for example, always using the right hand, or the left, or sometimes one hand and then the other.

It's common for boys to think they're doing it too much, but "too much" is a purely arbitrary phrase, with no meaning. Boys naturally masturbate a great deal in adolescence, as the powerful sex urge boils up in them. When they develop a sexual relationship with another person, or possibly several others, masturbation then becomes less important, although many still practice it from time to time if something turns them on and they're alone. Recently both men and women have learned that masturbation of various kinds can be a satisfying part of intercourse.

In later life there seems to be renewed interest in

masturbation, which may continue for some time, and so a cycle is completed. Boys come on strong in their adolescence, masturbate less as a rule in their twenties, thirties, and forties, then at some later date, return to it again with renewed interest.

It's also possible to use various objects for masturbation. Most common is a toilet paper tube or some other round object—a bottle with a wide mouth, for instance. Sometimes a boy uses a condom—a rubber contraceptive—which simulates the female vagina, although this isn't likely to satisfy a boy who has had actual intercourse.

Boys often think that whatever method they use is peculiar to them, maybe even something they've invented, and are quite surprised to learn later that others are using the same technique, whatever it is. In the search for sexual pleasure, the human male has thought of just about everything. Some like to insert a finger in the anus while they masturbate. Others even try to insert something into the end of the penis, but that is quite painful because the inside of the penis is very sensitive, and there is also a real danger that the object may carry germs inside and cause an infection or may be pushed inside too far and will have to be removed surgically.

At some time or other, it occurs to most boys to try to put their penises inside their own mouths. About one in every hundred succeeds. For the others it's anatomically impossible, as they soon discover to their frustration. Even if achieved, it doesn't usually become a major method of masturbation.

In short, it doesn't matter what method is used as long as no injury is caused to the penis, or no infection is introduced into it. Neither does it matter how often it's done. It isn't possible to masturbate to "excess," as doctors once believed. The body knows what "excess" really means. It sets its own limits. When a boy has masturbated a great deal, he will be temporarily unable to have an erection. That means he has reached his particular limit for the time being; the body has to rest for a while. But a young body restores itself very quickly, and a boy knows when it's restored because he'll be able to have an erection again.

If a boy studies his own masturbation habits, he'll observe that he's more likely to masturbate during times of tension and anxiety, like the period before examinations or when he's worried about some other problem. Then it becomes a good thing because masturbation is one of the best reducers of tension. Some athletes even do it before games if they are excessively anxious or tense. There's no truth in the old idea, still believed by many coaches and trainers, that masturbation makes a boy "weaker" and therefore less able to compete. I knew a track star who went out and set a national record within an hour after he had masturbated.

There's another side of that coin, though. As everybody in sports knows, tension can be helpful to an athlete in giving his best performance; there's such a thing as being too relaxed. Team members, in fact, are brought along carefully by the coaches to a peak of group tension before a game. It's only when there's too much tension, enough to hinder performance, that masturbation can be a help.

We don't hear much about one aspect of masturbation, but it ought to be mentioned because it has such a direct bearing on a boy's later sex life. When he begins to have intercourse, he often encounters a common problem—that is, delaying his ejaculation until the girl has her orgasm. Most girls take longer than boys do; consequently a boy may find it helpful to learn to delay his own orgasm when he masturbates during adolescence. It's not only helpful in that way but obviously adds to his own pleasure.

Many boys learn how to work themselves up nearly to the point of orgasm, then slow down and hold back for a while, continue until they nearly come once more, and so on until the orgasm is delayed indefinitely. Some learn to wait for a half hour or more, a much longer time than would usually be required in actual intercourse.

If he makes no attempt to delay, a boy finds himself coming in anywhere from a few seconds to a few minutes. A delay of five to ten minutes, or even longer, if he can learn to do it, will probably be useful later on in intercourse.

Another part of masturbation we don't hear much about is the fantasy or daydream I mentioned earlier that usually accompanies it. Oddly enough, many boys worry unnecessarily over what they think about while they're masturbating.

The sex urge is very powerful, and when a boy is excited, he's likely to have sexual thoughts about all kinds of things that ordinarily he wouldn't think of at all. Later the memories of what he thought may horrify him and make him feel guilty or afraid when he recalls them again after he ejaculates. It may help to know that most boys have one or more of these fantasies at one time or another, and having them doesn't mean they're abnormal or that they're losing their minds or that they should feel guilty for having them.

What are some of these fantasies? Remember, not every boy has them—many are afraid to, or haven't learned how, or don't have a very rich fantasy life at any time.

Fantasy, or daydreaming, takes many forms during masturbation. It happens just as easily when a boy is sitting at his desk in school, or walking home, or doing anything else. Some boys get their daydreams from stories they've been reading or pictures they've looked at. Often they make up their own stories or pictures and center on things they'd like to do sexually. Often boys are so imaginative in their daydreams that they think of things they would never do or even contemplate doing in reality. For instance, they might have fantasies of having sex with their sisters, a teacher, or even their mothers or fathers. Sometimes they imagine an orgy in which several boys and girls, or just boys, are taking part. At other times, it's having sex with a particular boy or girl, or even a grown man or woman. They may think about forcing someone else to have sex with them, or of being forced themselves.

These daydreams needn't be (and usually aren't) any more harmful than the common daydreams boys have about being the best baseball player in the world or becoming a millionaire, or any other kind of daydream that's beyond the limits of reality. The only harm that can come from them is guilt, or worry because of having such daydreams. This is an important lesson: Don't confuse fantasy with reality. A boy knows he has one chance in several million of becoming the world's greatest baseball or football player, and when he isn't daydreaming, he knows those are the odds. Just the same, he likes to imagine it sometimes.

That's the way it is with whatever fantasy a boy has when he's masturbating. The odds against the possibility that any of these fantasies might ever come true are extremely high, but it's exciting to think about them while he's doing it. Afterward he comes back to the real world and deals with it in a realistic way.

Most boys with the usual amount of curiosity wonder whether girls masturbate. They do, although maybe not quite so much as boys. Most females do so at some time during their lives, and today, when women are much more conscious of their sexuality and feel more free to express it, the number is probably quite high. In earlier estimates, less than a third of girls were supposed to have masturbated at all by age fifteen, when nearly all boys were doing it, but today this figure would have to be revised upward substantially because of greater knowledge and acceptance.

Girls have more ways of masturbating than boys do, but most of them do it in basically much the same way. They have a fleshy organ that is like a miniature penis, located just above the entrance to the vagina (where the penis is inserted in intercourse). It's called the clitoris. Looking like a small pea at the end of a slit, it's sexually very sensitive to the touch. Stimulated by a finger or hand, it becomes erect and eventually the girl has an orgasm, just as the boy does, except that she doesn't secrete any semen.

Recent studies show that no two women practice masturbation exactly alike. Most don't concentrate on the clitoris alone but stimulate the whole area of the sexual organ, because it's painful for them to manipulate the clitoris directly with too much pressure or for too long a time.

Since the clitoris is located between folds of flesh, it can also be stimulated in a way impossible for a boy. A girl can cross her legs tightly, and by swinging one of them, rubbing her thighs together against the clitoris, produce an orgasm. Some girls also do it by rubbing against an object, like the corner of a chair. Others do it in the bathtub, or under the shower, letting a stream of water flow against the sensitive clitoris. Or they may lie on their stomachs, or on a partner's buttocks, or on a pillow or with bedclothes between their legs, rubbing the clitoris against the object to attain orgasm.

Most girls, however, use the finger or the whole hand while lying either on their backs or on their stomachs. Some use objects to stimulate themselves— flashlights, bananas, cucumbers, or round cylinders— and insert such an object into their vaginas like a penis and push it in and out vigorously. Recently the vibrator has come into much more general use for this purpose.

Both boys and girls often masturbate because of conflicts in their lives that are not sexual. If they're bored or frustrated or lonely or have a poor opinion of themselves, or if they don't know how to get along with the opposite sex, or if they're in constant conflict with their parents or feel under heavy pressure at school—any one of these conditions may cause boys (or girls) to masturbate more than they might otherwise. Masturbation relieves their tension temporarily, but it's important for them to get some counseling help so their problems can be straightened out.

When we talk about such things as masturbation, we have to keep reminding ourselves that we're living in a society that's still in transition from long-established ways of thinking about sex to a freedom that hasn't been known before in this country, and hasn't yet, by any means, embraced everyone. People still differ about sexual subjects; otherwise, we wouldn't have legislative bodies and courts telling us what we can or can't do with our bodies. Whether they have the right to do so is not a subject for argument here. They *do* have the power to do it, and when they exercise this power, the result is much more likely to be repression than freedom. We have to remember that the dominant view in society, especially among parents, is still conservative.

Like everyone else, boys have to figure out their own relationship to this kind of society. Among other things, in accepting their own sexuality—particularly masturbation—they must understand the attitudes of other people. With understanding comes toleration of other viewpoints. Those attitudes aren't going to change overnight, and outright rebellion only aggravates situations that are better avoided.

For example, your parents may have the old attitudes about masturbation. They may never have mentioned the word to you, but you'll remember how, from your early childhood days, you learned to keep it secret from them. Long ago, too, you learned that it was something you could do in private. And that's the best policy. Whatever parents may think of masturbation, or even if you don't know *what* they think, it's something you do by yourself for your own enjoyment, privately and without any guilt feelings.

I've already pointed out that if you're being brought up in a religious faith, it will probably take a negative attitude toward sex, any sex, unless it's married sex. Eventually you'll have to decide for yourself how much you want to conform to the sexual code laid down by your faith. That will have much to do with masturbation and everything else you do sexually.

Looking at it from a nonreligious standpoint, I've tried to make clear in this chapter that masturbation is not only harmless but is positively good and healthy, an experience boys will find useful in their later sex lives and something they're going to do anyway. They should enjoy it as much as possible. You've learned here that every individual growing up has to learn what is acceptable public behavior and what is only acceptable in private. But don't let anyone tell you that "private" means "inferior" or "bad" or "dirty." Private masturbation is an entirely acceptable way of releasing sexual tension, besides being a joy and a satisfaction in itself and an important part of growing up. It can harm you only if it arouses feelings of guilt, anxiety, or fear. Don't let that happen.

CHAPTER · 5

Getting to Know Girls

Going out with girls begins to happen for most boys around age eleven, although there's plenty of variation. That's the age when what we call puberty usually sets in. If you've already been through it, you know the symptoms. A boy grows taller faster than he did before, and he'll continue to grow until he's about eighteen or twenty. (Please don't forget the ages I'm giving you here are averages; some boys begin to grow earlier than eleven, others not until they're fourteen or fifteen or even later.)

Other changes occur once the puberty process starts. At about twelve, usually, hair begins to grow around the penis, and soon after that, under the arms. At about thirteen, a boy will be able to ejaculate, and most boys do that as soon as they're able. This hap-

pens mostly through masturbation, but it can also occur as the result of wet dreams, fondling and kissing a
girl for a period of time, actual intercourse, or during
sex play with other boys. The boy's voice will change,
dropping to a lower register and often "cracking" in
the process. His breasts become sensitive, too, and he
may feel little hard knots beneath the nipples, which
go away in a few weeks or months.

Ordinarily these pubertal changes are spread out
over a period of two years or so. They may be happening to you now, or perhaps they've occurred quite
recently. But there's a more subtle change, too. You
may have had a good many sexual feelings before, with
erection and even orgasm, but when puberty arrives,
all these feelings will be stronger and more frequent.

At this point, boys develop a real interest in girls
for the first time, and it is now that they should be
aware that their ability to ejaculate injects an entirely
new element into their relationship with them. No
doubt boys are acutely aware that the girls have been
developing too. They go through much the same kind
of thing boys do, except for the change in voice. Another difference is in growth. Girls usually start shoot-
ing up about a year before boys, and this sometimes
creates a strange, even an embarrassing situation if a
boy finds his girl friend suddenly towering over him. It
might take two or three years to get things even again.

The bad news is that the time girls are getting
ahead of boys in height is just about the time when
boys first want to go out with them. Obviously, that
creates a problem. Girls often don't want to go out

with a boy who's shorter. If this happens to you, the problem can be handled by going out with younger girls who haven't started to grow yet, or else picking out girls your own age who are naturally shorter. Not all of them grow tall, by any means. There is also another alternative—go out with a girl who's broad-minded enough not to mind the difference in height, if it doesn't make any difference to you.

There are other contrasts in the way boys and girls grow up. For example, the hair around the sex organ of the girl tends to grow somewhat earlier than the boy's, and her breasts begin to enlarge earlier than breast knots appear in the boy. On the average, she also begins to menstruate about a year before the boy can ejaculate. But from his very first ejaculation, the boy has sperm in his semen and he can make a girl pregnant. There *is* some evidence to show that girls don't ovulate—that is, produce egg cells—at the time of their first menstruation, and in fact that may not happen until several months later. But even if this delay occurs, it isn't true of all girls, and none of them (or boys either) should take a chance.

A fact that's even more important in the way it differs between sexes, and one that may particularly puzzle a boy, is that even when all these changes have taken place in a girl's body, and she looks almost mature, she may not yet be terribly interested in sex, as a boy is almost certain to be. It's true that girls at this period find themselves more interested in boys in a way they hadn't been before, but they're likely to think of it as just the fun of going out and having a good time. Most don't want to go beyond that for a while, but at the same time, a boy is sexually excited by girls and feels the urge to ejaculate, even though he may not realize exactly what he's feeling.

The complication—and often trouble—comes when a girl doesn't know or understand how a boy feels at this particular time in his life. Sometimes girls are surprised to discover how much they're arousing boys by mutual fondling and kissing. To them it may mean no more than a special kind of friendship, and they don't think of what they're doing as sexual.

You may have experienced this scene yourself. You've gone out with a girl for an evening at the movies, or a party, and afterward you've taken her home, or you're sitting somewhere in the car, and you want to go on further with what probably began earlier in the evening—holding hands, touching, putting an arm around her shoulders, maybe even a quick kiss. Now you want to go further and you put your hand on her breast while you kiss her, or perhaps touch her thighs. By that time, your penis is erect, and you feel a strong impulse to go on somehow to the point of ejaculation.

But ask yourself what the girl may be thinking and feeling while this is going on. A girl of your own age or younger in that situation may not be aroused at all. (If she is, that's another story, and we'll talk about it later.) She may be thinking that all this pawing around is going to get her messed up, or if she's at home, a parent will come in and find her; in any case she may be thinking, "This boy may be a nice guy, but what does he think he's trying to do?" More likely, she *knows* what he's trying to do, and for one reason or another she isn't going to let it happen. Girls also wonder what a boy is going to tell the other boys about their evening together.

In this scene, chances are that if you try to go any further, she'll stop you and be angry, or at least resist you firmly, or the whole thing may disintegrate into embarrassment on both sides. It will be clear that you and the girl haven't been operating on the same wavelength at all, and you will be puzzled and frustrated. Worse, you may feel rejected and hurt, and the experience may hamper you in getting to the same point next time you go out with a girl. If it's the same girl, the situation could be even worse; the fear of rejection is powerful. If you're rejected more than once, it's possible you'll begin to feel there is something wrong with you, and that could lead to psychological problems. And all because you didn't understand why she made you stop.

But it isn't only the failure to understand each other sexually that makes trouble in these early relationships. There are a good many other differences between boys and girls, and the fear both sexes have in common is the fear of being turned down, of rejection. Millions sit beside the telephone and don't make the call they want to make because of that fear.

You'll have to fight the fear of rejection right from the beginning because it can spoil a lot of good times and opportunities. It may help to remember that you're in the same boat with everybody else. All of us, young or old, are going to be rejected during our lives

—when we look for jobs, in relationships with other people, including sexual ones, and at countless other times. We simply have to learn how to deal with rejection in its many shapes and forms so that it won't hurt us too much.

You can learn to do it in several ways. And there is one way *not* to deal with it—by turning your back on life and trying to avoid placing yourself in a position where you *might* be rejected. That would be like shutting yourself up in a room for the rest of your life. You could do it, but life wouldn't be life anymore. It's far better to figure out why you've been rejected, if it happens, and then try to do something about it. It could be *your* fault, you know; maybe you did something wrong. But even then, you can learn from the experience and not repeat it.

Most often, though, the problem is with the girl who rejects you. She may be interested in you for selfish reasons, not you as a person. For instance, she may be going out with you only because she wants to go to a particular party and no one else has asked her. Next time you call, she may say no simply because you don't fit in with her new plans, and in that case, there's nothing wrong with you. She's thinking only of herself, in a thoughtless and rude way, to be sure, but that's her privilege.

Again, a girl may turn you down not because there's anything wrong with you but simply because she just isn't interested in you. That may hurt your ego, but just remember that *you're* not interested in every girl you meet. If she rejects you, and you can't find anything in your own behavior to account for it, the best thing is to understand that it's her right and privilege to feel that way—and look for somebody else.

But let's not underestimate the feeling. It hurts to be rejected, and it's possible there's even more rejection today than there used to be, in this speeded-up world we live in, which is filled with more possibilities than your parents ever enjoyed. At the same time, it's true that the feeling of rejection, of not being wanted, is one of the most devastating things that can happen to a person—and don't forget, it happens to girls, too. Rejection is the price you pay for learning to get along with girls, by being with them, by going out with them while you're young.

It may be consoling to remember that everybody makes mistakes in this department, and if you don't take yourself too seriously, you can even laugh at some of your own. In any case, it's absolutely true that a "failure" in this area isn't the end of the world. If you learn to deal with rejection in going out, it will help you to handle it in other situations as you grow up to be an adult. It's like learning any other skill. Once learned, it's something that will always be useful, a help in getting over rough spots.

Probably the best way to begin is by learning to relate to girls—that is, by being really interested in another person, being concerned about her and her interests. We may be living in the selfish "me era," but it's as true now as it ever was that you can't build good relationships on that idea. To relate, you have to accept the fact that another person has the right to reject you, and you have the same right. No one is obligated to accept anyone else. If you can understand and accept that right, which everyone possesses, you won't be nearly so hurt when rejection happens to you.

Of course, you may try to relate to a girl with the best of intentions, but in doing so you may make all kinds of mistakes. Everybody does. For instance, you may do something you know is awkward—you may make a careless remark that offends the girl. Or you may fail to introduce her to someone you know when you meet at a party. Or leave her alone to talk to someone else when you're the one who's brought her to the party. Or you may find yourself in a situation that's beyond your experience, and that may make you stutter and stammer around trying to handle it. Even more common, a boy may be so interested in himself that he doesn't think about a girl's feelings, of what *she* may want to do, or what *she* may like to talk about. All too commonly, boys (and grown men) may not want to listen to girls (or women); they just want to talk about themselves.

An even more common kind of behavior that leads to rejection occurs when a boy waits too long to ask a girl to go out, either because he's shy or else is afraid he'll be rejected. When he summons up his courage at last, calls her, and finds out someone else has asked her first, he's crushed. Logic may tell him that he might have expected this to happen, and that she meant no offense to him as an individual, but just the same he feels rejected—maybe unworthy, too.

All mistakes are profitable in the end, however, if you can learn from them. It's not necessarily a bad thing to make mistakes.

Sometimes it happens that boys are prodded into going out with girls too early, before they're really ready for it. Parents who do this don't realize that a boy can be miserable if he hasn't grown up quite as fast as some of his friends and doesn't yet have the interest in girls that they do. He may get some prodding from his friends, too, who are going out with girls and invite him along to be part of the crowd. That's especially hard to resist, but if a boy isn't ready, he shouldn't go out with girls until he is. There's plenty of time.

When he does begin to go out, he may find it easier to go with another couple or with a group. That makes conversation less difficult while he's learning how to get along with girls and is acquiring a little assurance about being with them. This works best if the other boys in the group are in the same situation. In that case, they'll be reinforcing each other. If one is more experienced, the others can learn by watching how he behaves. But after a boy has done this a few times, he's likely to have learned enough to go out with a particular girl—and by then he has probably found a particular girl he wants to go out with.

If what I've said here doesn't seem to apply to your particular case, that's because there are so many social differences affecting adolescent boys. These differences are as great as the physical ones. America is a big country, with people living in all kinds of situations, and the way they live varies from place to place, so going out with girls isn't the same in big cities as it is in small towns, nor is it the same in different parts of big cities.

Young people in California have different lifestyles from those in a small town in Maine. Even the look-alike suburbs in our country may have different behavior patterns, depending on where they are. Geography, family backgrounds—these and a lot of other things make a difference. So it isn't safe to make sweeping generalizations; people behave differently depending on where and how they live.

One of the major differences is using the family car. This raises all kinds of problems in small towns and other places where the car is essential equipment. But in New York, for instance, boys and girls have an entirely different set of problems, since not many of their parents are likely to have cars. If the city is Los Angeles, however, a car is just as essential as though people lived in the country.

Where you live, in short, has a lot to do with how you go out with girls, and how you learn to relate to them. For example, it's easier to have sexual activity if you have a car, and consequently this freedom often creates conflicts with parents, especially in the case of girls. But parents worry not only about what might occur sexually; they know the high rate of fatal automobile accidents among young people and the dangers of drinking at parties. Consequently the whole learning experience becomes more complicated. Combining freedom and cars, as we seem to be doing today, makes the possibilities for getting into trouble as numerous as those for learning.

The most common difficulty occurs in small towns where, even with cars, there aren't many places to go out with a girl. This situation only multiplies the problems, since adolescents are not likely to be sitting home every night reading a good book or listening to the radio or watching television. The pregnancy rate is high in such places, but then, so is it in uncontrolled urban environments.

When Kinsey gathered his statistics in the 1940s, they showed that four out of ten boys had intercourse outdoors some of the time, and about the same proportion had it in a girl's home. For about one in ten, the place was a car, and for about the same proportion it was in the boy's home. The most infrequent places were hotels, motels, and the beach. While no reliable statistics are available today, it's unlikely that these figures have changed substantially.

Family backgrounds often make a difference. Sometimes religion may dictate not only what girls a boy may go out with, but even how often he is permitted to go out with them. Again, some parents are overfearful and do their best to restrict their children; others don't seem to be worried about what their sons and daughters are doing and appear to believe that what they don't know won't hurt them. In the homes of divorced parents, it can go either way—too much or too little restriction, depending on the situation. Boys and girls in such situations are likely to start going out sooner than others and to have earlier sexual experiences. Ethnic differences, too, may determine how much the weight of tradition will affect these early learning experiences. Today, it should be added, there are far fewer restrictions than there were in your parents' day. Standards change from generation to generation, and now, obviously, there's a great deal more freedom than there has ever been. Parents may still be debating whether this is a good or a bad thing, but very few adolescents (except those who are religiously motivated) would argue against their freedom.

In any case, all other things being equal, a boy who has been going out with girls for a while tends to find a particular girl. When that happens, an old question arises. It used to be called "going steady," but now it doesn't have a name; it just means going out with one person on a regular basis. Parents may still argue about whether such exclusivity is a good thing at such an early age, but adolescents themselves don't consider it an arguable subject.

It's easy enough to see why it can be a good thing. Seeing only one person offers a certain security. Both the boy and the girl know they've always got someone to go out with. Since the girl is not going with anyone else, she's always available for the boy, as he is for her, which is just as important as far as she's concerned.

From a boy's standpoint it's a relief not to have to make a new adjustment to someone else every time he goes out, nor does he have to meet new parents. He likes the girl very much, probably believes he's in love with her, and it's a satisfaction to be with the girl he thinks is more attractive than any other he knows. It's a deeper and more emotional relationship than either can obtain by simply playing the field, and of course that's what marriage is about. Rarely will a boy marry this particular girl, but he'll be getting a valuable lesson in what marriage is like, in what it means to be with someone all the time in a close relationship.

But there are also some advantages in *not* going out with the same person all the time. If you go out with a lot of different girls instead of concentrating on one, you'll get to know a wide variety, and in time you'll have a better idea of what kind of personality you get along with best—an excellent preparation for marriage or any other kind of committed relationship.

These early friendships duplicate to some extent the problems of such close relationships in later life. A boy goes out with a girl, let's say, who is moody and irritable, or has a sharp temper, and they have frequent fights. He's likely to be wary of that kind of girl later on. Again, he may find out that his girl friend is too sloppy in dress and manners for the kind of taste he's acquired, and that will be another kind of guide. If a girl is careless about what she says, if she's tactless and doesn't care how her words affect other people, a boy will be able to see at first hand how hard it is to live with that kind of person. But if he finds a girl who is warm and loving and sympathetic, even though he probably won't marry her, he will have had the experience of knowing what it's like to be with such a person.

Girls have the same learning opportunities as boys, of course. When they do marry, both may make mistakes, but it won't be the result of inexperience. Early adolescent relationships are often painful because they constantly break up, and new combinations are tried, but it's all a part of the tumult of growing up. It's how we learn—if we do.

Everyone knows that people *do* fall in love with others who have the bad traits I've mentioned above, and simply disregard them, but it's also true that earlier experiences are bound to affect choices in a way a boy, or a girl, may not even be conscious of, and can influence decisions in subtle ways, often indirectly.

There's still another good reason for a boy to go out with a lot of different girls instead of confining himself to one. It will be valuable experience because he'll be placed in a variety of social situations, meeting new friends, meeting new parents, and all of this will help him to construct his own social life later on.

No boy who thinks he's fallen in love at an early age will ever believe it, but if he concentrates on one girl for a long time to the exclusion of everyone else, he's virtually certain to wake up one day and discover there are a great many other kinds of girls in the world, and a lot of different experiences, sexual and otherwise, he could have been having if he hadn't concentrated on one girl. It's hard to realize at the time, but it *is* a shame to miss so much of life before settling down to the realities of being an adult. Someone once said that youth is wasted on the young, and it's true that there are those who don't take full advantage in the brief time they have it. Such youthful freedom is unlikely to come again. Marriages in adolescence are too often robbers of life.

As boys today know, what usually happens is that both they and the girls have a lot of different relationships before they settle on one, if they do. There are all sorts of variations, and I wouldn't be so foolish as to prescribe any kind of exact formula for going out, or for getting married, either. Most boys discover that their friends—and they themselves, by and large—go along on some kind of middle ground, with periods of going out steadily with one girl interrupted by other periods of playing around.

Of course the problems of going out are not the only ones adolescents have. It's an unusual boy or girl who doesn't have some kind of friction with his parents along the way. Some of these conflicts are the usual family arguments that seem so important at the time but are really trivial in the long run—like who's going to get the car on a particular night. But other troubles may be deeper, and when they occur, they're most often centered on the inability of parents to realize their children are growing up and don't want to be treated like children, and on the other side, the tendency of young people to think they are more grown-up than they really are.

A twelve- or thirteen-year-old boy who is treated like one by his parents will be fourteen before long, and that short time may make a considerable difference in him. But all too often, his parents continue to treat him as though he hadn't yet slipped out of childhood.

It's a wise parent who can keep up with a growing boy or girl. Admittedly, it isn't easy. Parents have to keep shifting ground, for one thing, and that's always difficult. The point here is that a boy shouldn't be surprised if he's treated by his parents as younger than he actually is. It's hard for them—and for him, too—to determine sensibly when he's "old enough" to go out with girls, or stay out late, or drive the car. Parents are inclined to be especially reluctant to realize that a boy is "old enough" to be interested in sex and girls.

So what can be done about this very old and difficult conflict? Quite a bit. First of all, a boy needs to realize that the conflict is a part of growing up, and that's a process hard on both parents and children at times. Adults often say a boy should be responsible and show them he's "old enough," and the boy's easy answer to that one is to ignore it, simply because it's an adult's way of thinking, and in particular a parent's way.

If a boy stops to think of it, though, it *does* make sense. Very soon he'll have to demonstrate he's "old enough" to do other things, like showing he's responsible enough to be in college, to hold a job, and somewhere along the line, to take the responsibility for looking after another human being, in marriage or whatever kind of relationship he works out.

It's easy to demonstrate responsibility in adolescence. The method is very simple. It's done by easy stages. Let's say your parents ask you to be home at a certain hour when you go out at night. If you persist in disobeying this relatively small request, your parents can hardly be blamed if they don't find you responsible in larger matters. But on the other hand, if you show you can be depended upon to do this one small thing, then your area of responsibility can be gradually extended to other things. If you show that you're responsible about handling money, whether it's from an allowance or a part-time job, chances are your parents will take a much more lenient view if you need more money later on to go out with girls.

What do you have to do to prove you're responsible? Just show that you're reliable, that you'll do what you have to do, whether it's homework or some household chore or whatever it is, and that you'll do it without being nagged—another quick source of irritation on both sides. Doing things on your own without being told is a badge of responsibility.

Since it's so easy to be responsible, it's too bad so many boys, probably most of them, insist on rebelling against their parents. Since "teen-age rebellion" is a cliché of modern life, teen-agers somehow think they don't have any choice. This leads to trouble in several areas, not the least of which is going out with girls. Boys go out with girls secretly, hoping their parents won't find out. Of course, not many parents would forbid it these days, but conflicts continue on other levels about such possibly sexual relationships. If you have this conflict, it comes down to a question of honesty. It might be a good thing to examine your own set of values and decide whether it's more important to be honest with your parents or go along with your friends and do what they're doing without saying anything.

Obviously, either way has its drawbacks. If you're honest, it may become difficult or impossible to do some of the things you want to do, and you may have to go counter to what other boys in your group are doing, which means losing face. But if you keep on lying at home, and going out with your friends to do whatever you want to do, there are probably going to be more or less deep feelings of guilt, if you love your parents, and along with that, a fear of what may happen if you're caught. The important thing is to face the alternatives squarely and come to some kind of decision that doesn't waffle between the two.

Adolescents are commonly ruled by what their peers do. They want to do whatever everybody else is doing, and of course it isn't easy *not* to go along with the gang, to assert your independence and refuse to be a sheep. But think about it. It may be better to be comfortable about yourself.

Even if there's no problem at home, there are some boys who just don't know how to begin going out with girls. It's a new experience, and they would be ashamed to ask advice from an older boy, or anyone else for that matter. Nobody wants to look as young and inexperienced as he really is.

For such boys, there's one essential in getting started: You begin relationships with girls by learning to talk to them. It's as simple as that. Talk to them in school, on the playground, or anywhere else you encounter them. Inevitably the talk will get around to the things you have in common—sports, movies, music, teachers, friends. That can lead easily to an invitation to enjoy some activity together. All you have to do then is to agree on a time and place, and you're on the way. But talking to a girl also implies listening to her, and you'll never find out what your common interests are if you don't let her talk about them so you can discuss them together. Girls of all ages like boys who listen to them.

It's important, too, as you start going out with girls, to remember what I was talking about earlier in this chapter—that girls may very often think of going out as nothing more than a social good time, without any idea of sexual activity taking place, while you may be thinking of it as a way of having some sort of physical contact with a girl. As a wise man said, "Girls think of sex as a way of getting love; boys think of love as a way of getting sex."

That may be true in a general way, but it doesn't mean everybody has to be so singleminded. Boys are perfectly capable of loving whether they get any sex or not, and girls may be loving but also very interested in sex. It depends. But this difference in attitude is more often true than not, and it accounts for many of the difficulties in boy-girl relationships. When it's carried over into adult life, it's responsible for a great deal of misunderstanding between men and women.

Just remember that physical contact may not be what's going through a girl's mind. Going out together is only a first step for both of you. In most cases, much else has to happen before sexual behavior takes place, if it does. You shouldn't draw hasty conclusions. If a girl holds your hand or puts her own hand on you, or even kisses you, it may not mean anything more than that she likes you.

Liking, however, can be the prelude to physical contact, and the more a girl gets to like a boy, the more she's interested in physical contact. And the more consideration a boy shows for her desires and feelings, the more she'll like him. It's surprising what a little consideration will do.

That may sound old-fashioned to you, something your parents might say. We live in a time when girls are very often attracted to boys who are anything but considerate, and often they tend to think of strong males as those who don't show much, if any, consideration for girls. More and more, too, young girls are asking, like their older sisters, to be treated as equals.

Much of all this, however, is on the surface. Underneath, a female may feel equal and want to be treated that way, but she also wants to be "courted" by the male, as she is in all human and animal societies. You may be cool, and play at being casual about sex and other human relationships, but just being cool won't lead to a real emotional relationship with a girl, and it isn't the way to have a lasting one.

True, it's an easier way to relate, but there's a great deal more to love and the living together it leads to. It's impossible to get the most satisfaction out of relationships with girls by thinking only of sex, or by playing it cool, either.

In essence, "cool" says: "I'm interested in myself, and if you don't want to come along with me, all right. If you don't, I don't care." Good relationships can't develop on that kind of foundation. They grow from mutual interests into a more intense and exclusive interest, until—if they're serious—they result in being together in every way. Even if they're not serious, good relationships develop in a give-and-take manner —two people giving of themselves to each other to the degree that each will accept. "Cool" is a static, don't-care state of being in which nothing much that is more than momentarily satisfying is likely to happen.

Don't forget. Penises and vaginas don't love each other. Only people can do that.

CHAPTER · 6

Learning About Sex with Girls

Eventually, as you start to grow up, you'll be having sexual encounters of one kind or another. So let's talk now about all kinds of physical contact short of intercourse. What is this very common activity, anyway? Actually, it's a way for two people to communicate. Usually it involves at least some degree of affection and emotional feeling and an interest, deep or not, in the other person. It can also be a launching stage into intercourse, although that may not occur. But since almost all intercourse does begin with this kind of mutual fondling, doing it becomes a learning experience in itself. No one who's doing it thinks of it in such academic terms, of course. It's simply pleasure for its own sake.

To do this with a girl is like developing a story plot, except that this story can end anywhere along the way without getting to the real end, which is intercourse. It begins when you put your arms around someone else —a hug, the oldest of human gestures. Then if nothing happens to interrupt it, the action goes from hugging to kissing to tongue kissing, to putting a hand on the breasts outside and then inside the clothing, sometimes with the mouth on the breasts at the same time. Finally, the hands of one or both people will be on the sex organs of the other outside the clothing, then inside. A boy may put his mouth on the girl's vagina, or she may put hers on his penis, or they may do this at the same time. That usually is leading up to intercourse, although it can also occur without going as far as intercourse.

Girls tend to draw the line at some point or other during this progression I've described, but most people engage in all, or at least part, of this behavior before marriage or during adolescence whether intercourse occurs or not.

If you haven't begun to do any of these things yet, you may be wondering, "Why do people do this, anyway?" There are three good reasons. The most obvious is that it's so much fun. But there's a big difference here between boys and girls. Boys can be aroused by thinking about sex, or seeing something sexual, before actual contact arouses them still more. Girls, however, particularly when they're growing up, aren't usually excited by looking at "dirty pictures" or hearing talk about sex, or even thinking about it—at least not as much or as easily as boys. Both sexes are aroused by physical contact, and they meet on that common ground. So fondling is fun for both boys and girls, and for boys especially because they're further excited by the knowledge that the girl is aroused.

Some parts of the body are more easily stimulated than others, and naturally those are the ones both sexes want to touch. All these areas have a great many nerve endings that convey sexual excitement in a very complicated way through the brain centers that control them. Kissing, for example, is pleasurable partly because the tongue and the inner part of the lips have many nerve endings.

There's more to it than physiology, though. We can see that when we consider the meaning different societies attach to a kiss, that most elementary form of body contact. In some parts of the world people regard kissing as disgusting. They get just as much pleasure out of rubbing their noses together. In America kissing in public was something people didn't do unless they were related. Now it's common with everyone, and even in high school corridors students don't pay much attention, if any, when boys and girls kiss each other. Motion pictures are full of kinds of kissing, much of which would never have been seen fifty years ago, but in India it is uncommon in movies made there and is deplored in American imports by some Indians. Kissing in public is rarely seen there. In fact, most of the peoples of the world don't enjoy kissing the way we do in the Western nations, where almost everybody thinks of it as a pleasure.

Lips are the most obvious zone of sexual pleasure and the one most commonly employed, but there are other parts of the body that are easily stimulated sexually. Rubbing or kissing the nipples of the breast will do it. So will stroking the clitoris and the opening of the vagina. As any boy knows, the penis is very easy to stimulate. But almost any area of the body can produce sexual feelings in a particular individual. There are cases on record in which girls have achieved orgasm by rubbing the lobes of their ears.

Another reason people like physical contact with each other, besides the fact that it's fun, is because it's useful as a learning experience before they're ready for actual intercourse—although I'm sure no adolescent looks at it that way. A boy needs to know how to stimulate a girl properly, as well as how to stimulate himself, beginning with kissing and going on to the more involved techniques, as a preparation for intercourse.

But is "technique" really necessary? Doesn't a boy learn just by doing what comes naturally? Most adults think so. The answer, however, is both yes and no. True, he learns by trial and error, according to his own personality. Techniques are best learned by not concentrating first on intercourse. Fondling each other is just the preliminary. But there's no need to get hung up on that word "technique," because it isn't all that complicated or involved. Most boys have a great time while they're learning.

Another reason people like to fondle each other is that it's a form of communication. There's a lot of meaning in it. But it won't be very meaningful unless it's mutual. To show loving feelings for a girl, physically, when she isn't able to accept them isn't the kind of communication that will help anyone build a relationship. Most boys, after they're aroused, get so interested in their own excitement that they forget about the girl's response and may not even care whether she's responding or not. In a situation like that, communication between the two isn't possible.

Maybe it will help you to understand what happens if I point out some of the other differences between boys and girls. Girls aren't as easily aroused as boys, and aren't necessarily aroused by the same things. A boy can get excited just thinking about what he'd like to do with a girl, or maybe by the memory of what he's done with her before, or even by sitting close to her. For most girls, it's pleasant enough to have such thoughts and memories, or even to have the boy sitting very close, but that doesn't necessarily mean she's sexually stimulated. In that case, if a boy starts to fondle her, he will be much more aroused than she is, and he needs to slow down, to let her come at her own pace to his state of arousal—if she does.

Many girls know without being told what these differences are, and they act accordingly, which quite often frustrates the boy. They often hesitate to begin because they know they'll be aroused by physical contact if it goes on long enough. If boys show them erotic pictures, mistakenly thinking it's going to excite them, they are usually not only unexcited but sometimes repelled, and the boy wastes his attempt and may even offend the girl.

Girls are much more affected by the right setting, and by what has gone on between the two before physical contact begins. A long evening of talking and feeling close to someone, enjoying a movie or a party together, and then being together in some intimate setting will much more easily prepare the way for contact. The "Okay, baby, let's go" approach some boys use is a definite turn-off for most girls, especially if it comes early and without warning. Girls also don't want physical contact shortly after an argument, or in a situation where they might be embarrassed, especially one where they might be discovered. All these things are much more upsetting to most girls than they are to boys. Let me say that I'm talking here about the usual girl and boy. There are a lot of exceptions, and you or your girl friend may be among them.

Whatever the circumstances, when a boy does get around to fondling a girl, he'll find himself very much aroused sexually. His penis will be erect for a long period of time, or it will be alternately erect and soft during a long period of contact. If the erection lasts for a long time, he may have what seems like an ache in the groin, or in his sex organ. A boy thinks the pain is in his testicles, but it's much more likely to be a cramp in the muscles of the groin, where the legs join the abdomen. It can be uncomfortable, but it's nothing to worry about.

Relief is easy. Many boys masturbate as soon as they can after a session with a girl that doesn't end in orgasm, and that will relieve the ache. These days, however, there are more and more girls willing to stimulate a boy to the point of orgasm without having intercourse with him—they use this as a substitute. It can be done two ways: either he lies on or against the girl and goes through the motions of intercourse, or else she masturbates him.

If the fondling goes on long enough, the girl may become as aroused as the boy and may be just as frustrated if intercourse—for whatever reason—doesn't happen. If she's aroused enough, she too may want to get release from sexual tension, and in that case, the boy should help her—remembering, though, that it isn't always possible to judge the state of a girl's arousal by his own. She may not have progressed as much as he thinks she has. It takes experience to know how close a girl may be to orgasm. The usual signs are a warm, moist skin, rapid breathing, and a tense body.

Girls respond to sexual stimulation in a variety of ways. Some are aroused quickly and easily. Others are slow because of various fears and inhibitions. There are a few who are never aroused at all, even as adults. Some girls permit physical contact not because they're aroused or even want to be, but because they think a boy won't be interested in them anymore if they don't. Consequently the better a boy is able to judge why a girl is letting him fondle her, the better he'll be able to decide how far he should try to go. If she responds to his kissing and touching spontaneously and eagerly, it's a good sign she wants the physical contact as much as he does.

Since drinking became so much more common among adolescents, boys have inherited the old myth held by their fathers, too, that alcohol is the best way to stimulate a girl to sex. That's because the boy is thinking only of himself. He knows that when he drinks, he becomes more uninhibited and amorous, and he believes (mistakenly) that he is more alert and sensitive to stimulation of all kinds, so he thinks (again mistakenly) that he and a girl can drink themselves right into a sexual situation.

That may happen, but only to a limited extent. It's true that alcohol removes inhibitions—to a point. But the fact is that it's a depressant, not a stimulant. Even a small amount—a single drink or two—depresses the higher nervous centers; it depresses the things that inhibit the individual and gives him the illusion of being more stimulated. But if you add only a little more alcohol, the lower nervous centers are also depressed, and a boy (or an adult) will then not be capable of functioning, sexually or otherwise, as well as he did before. This means that the more a boy drinks, the longer it will take him to get an erection and ejaculate.

You've heard a girl being called a "cockteaser," I'm sure. That's someone who enjoys getting a boy aroused and then doesn't do anything about it, who backs off and leaves him frustrated rather than coming to orgasm. There are several kinds of these girls. With some, this behavior is unconscious. Either out of inexperience or ignorance, they don't understand what they're doing. They don't know how easy it is to arouse a boy, and they're often indignant and astonished when he shows his frustration by aggressive behavior. Once all this is explained to these girls, they may understand and then decide more intelligently how much physical contact they want to have.

The second kind of girl is different. She knows very well what she's doing, but she keeps on doing it out of spite, malice, resentment, or some other personal reason. Some are actresses who play out this hostile little drama because they don't like males in general, and they choose this childish way to get even with them.

Then there are some who tease because other girls tell them it's a smart thing to do, and may even show them how to do it. Still others have an urge to dominate males, and they choose this method because it's a way of controlling boys and showing their aggression at the same time. I'm not at all sure that girls in this category can be made to change. If you encounter such a teaser, my best advice is simply to stop taking her out.

This whole business of physical contact, of fondling, is obviously not an easy matter. There's no question that it can be exhilarating, loving, and pleasurable. If a girl resists the boy, it may add to his stimulation, but at the same time it may be extremely unfair to her if he insists, and the whole thing may end in a bad scene. Many boys simply don't understand why girls aren't as aroused as they are. Often a boy may not even be aware that his partner isn't, or if he does know, he doesn't care, and he keeps right on with what he's trying to do, whether the girl wants it or not.

Some girls may like this aggressive kind of boy, but

most don't like it when he tries to force them into physical contact they don't want. After all, it's supposed to be a learning experience, and learning to dominate a girl physically is certainly not the way to build a satisfactory relationship of any kind. And it won't help to make a boy happier in his future relationships with girls.

Let's not lose sight of the fact that when they're growing up, most boys and girls fondle each other for the enjoyment and stimulation they get out of it. It also can't help being a kind of preparation for adult relationships. Like all the other areas in which one person deals with another, it isn't an act performed in a vacuum. Two people are always involved. One person's pleasure is not the only consideration, unless that person is an utterly selfish individual who doesn't care about anyone else.

Whenever there's another person to be thought of, responsibility begins. Clearly it's unfair for a girl to enjoy arousing a boy and then rejecting him, or making fun of him. In such cases, the boy should simply stop seeing her. He may think she's unfair, but at the same time, he doesn't have the right to force physical contact on her if she doesn't want it.

In any situation where fondling is involved, I think it helps if the boy remembers the differences in sexual nature I've been talking about in this chapter. He should be considerate of his partner, allow for her slower arousal, and not force her to do something she isn't ready for or doesn't want to do. But if the fondling is going to lead to orgasm, he should be certain that it happens to her as well as to him—if she wants it.

Such mutual consideration raises fondling from mere physical exercise, or aggressive behavior on one side or the other, to a communication of feelings and emotions that will be an immediate and continuing source of pleasure for two people and will also be an extremely valuable preparation for a satisfying adult relationship later on.

CHAPTER · 7

The Real Thing

It would be easy to believe that we're living in a time of complete sexual freedom if we judged by what we see in the movies and on television and read about in our daily papers. As your parents, or maybe your grandparents, will be glad to confirm, the old problems and restrictions are no more. But are they?

For instance, the undeniable fact that many more adolescents are actually having intercourse today, and that they take sexual matters far more casually, doesn't mean an orgy of youthful intercourse is taking place across the country. Some do, but many don't. Percentages may change, but the "do nots" still predominate. High school pregnancies are up sharply, but for every girl who gets pregnant, there are a hundred or more who have never had intercourse.

Parental attitudes have changed too, although that may be hard for some of you reading this to believe. Even though there has been a conservative backlash in the eighties, some parents, especially those in the middle and upper middle classes, are much more tolerant of their children's sexual behavior than they used to be. Unfortunately, for every mother and father who assume their daughter is going to have intercourse and see that she is equipped with some kind of contraceptive, there are many more who are extremely anxious and disturbed about the possibility and try to prevent it as much as they can. As for boys, too many parents still believe boys shouldn't, and therefore won't, have intercourse until they get married, in spite of all the evidence to the contrary.

Despite their own sophistication and acceptance of sex, adolescents are not all committed to taking full advantage of the freedom changing times have given them. Every girl doesn't want to have intercourse with boys simply because it's easier than it used to be, and boys who think all girls do are quite often surprised when the girl draws the line just before the actual act. The fact that contraceptives are now so easily available doesn't mean everyone is going to take advantage of them, even though a growing number of teen-agers understand the threat of AIDS.

In our day, virginity is not the great prize it once was (at one time it was exchanged only for matrimony); on the other hand, a substantial number of boys prefer to marry a virgin whether they expect to find one or not, and an even greater number of girls have no intention of taking advantage of their new opportunities for premarital intercourse. Of course, marriage itself is no longer the only alternative; living together is now commonplace.

Maybe you don't need a reminder, but I'm going to remind you anyway that if you want to have intercourse with girls, you're not likely to find much sympathy for this idea at home if your parents find out about it. Premarital sex may be common, but it isn't sanctioned either by law or by religious faiths. Things aren't changing quite as fast as we're led to believe.

What I want to talk about is not whether you should or should not have intercourse, but about some of the problems connected with it. One of the new factors to be considered is the changed and still changing status of women, which extends to their young sisters. Your grandmother grew up in a time when women had few rights, legal or otherwise. Many men treated their wives as an absolute tyrant would treat a slave, and some still do. For centuries before that, men regarded women as pieces of property to dispose of as they wished. From the time the colonies became the United States until relatively recently a woman could not vote, nor could she move about freely in society except at its lower levels. For the most part, she was expected to be a dutiful wife, to take care of home and children and obey her husband. Women who escaped male tyranny did so either by being as uncompromising as the men or by devious and deceptive behavior—what they called "getting around" a man.

All this began to change when women won the right to vote in 1920 and later began to be an increasingly important part of the work force. Today they constitute about half of that force, and not nearly as many think of themselves as housewives. The slogan today is "You can have it all," meaning a career and marriage, or an equivalent relationship.

Boys today are growing up in a world where women's struggle toward equality has made giant strides, but the old cry "It's a man's world" still has plenty of vitality. You'll notice this as you grow up in the new era, especially in sexual matters. As far as most boys are concerned, girls are still divided into two classes, those who will have intercourse and those who won't. Many of them have never heard of the hymen, that membrane surrounding the opening of the vagina, which was once the mark of virginity. We know now that it can be broken in other ways than by intercourse —through sports, riding horses, or masturbation, among other means. Still, the fact of permitting intercourse or not is the dividing line for both sexes.

That's the real question, not whether the hymen is broken. While there is still a surprising percentage of holdouts, more and more males are indifferent to whether their prospective brides or lovers are virgins or not, in any sense. Increasingly less important, too, is whether a couple has intercourse before they marry or start living together. The sticking point is whether to have it with someone you're not committed to, which may not bother adults but may be of concern to adolescents. Many adolescent girls indulge in other kinds of sexual behavior but feel they're not yet ready to have actual intercourse, for one reason or another. Sexual passion may sweep them into it before they are ready, but usually they think twice about crossing the line.

It's worth remembering that intercourse is never a casual thing, even though it may be taken casually at the time. Serious and long-range consequences can follow it, particularly if it results in pregnancy or in venereal disease. Even if none of these things is involved, doing this most intimate of acts can't help changing the nature of a relationship, and that raises the possibility of emotional and psychological damage. Of course, it can have just the opposite effect and give a big boost to your joy of living and your feelings of love and well-being.

No one is naive enough to think that if you're at the point of having intercourse, you'll be considering the consequences or wondering whether it's a good idea or not. At that moment all you want is the exciting, stimulating pleasure of it. You might feel the same anticipation before doing something else—playing a sport or going to a party, for instance—but intercourse is different because its intimacy and its meanings result in much greater enjoyment than any other activity.

Like any other pleasure, however, it isn't without its possible drawbacks. Particularly in adolescence it may be accompanied by strong feelings of guilt on one or both sides, and that will certainly detract from the pleasure. If you're doing it for the first time, you may also be surprised to find that it's a disappointment—not quite what you thought it was going to be. You may have had higher expectations—unimaginable ecstasy—than the act provides, contrary to what you may have read or seen in movies. Bells don't necessarily ring and rockets shoot off. It's possible that intercourse won't seem like anything more than a quick pleasure, like masturbation. For girls, it may not even be as good.

So if you don't expect too much, you won't be disappointed. This doesn't mean intercourse can't be all the marvelous things you imagined, but that isn't likely to happen until it's done by two people who have a warm, caring, loving relationship that is built on a solid foundation of previous friendship. Intercourse is what two people put into it. It is not a guaranteed rocket-launching experience for everybody.

If you're having sex with someone you have no intention of marrying or living with, it can be a good training ground for a more committed experience later on. It teaches what one of the most important aspects of living together is all about, so it's a good thing if you learn how to do it well. In a fundamental way, it's like learning to play a game. You have to learn the fundamentals first if you want to play it well.

For the adolescent boy and girl who start having intercourse with the idea that they will get married later on, it will be a big help in finding out if they're really compatible or not. Early marriages entered into on a wave of passion too often cool down and end in the face of everyday realities. It's like taking a car out on a test run before you buy it. If that sounds unromantic and without much feeling for the girl, remember there are many marriages in which two people find they're well suited to each other in every respect except sexually. It's better to find this out *before* the marriage ceremony than after.

But in these circumstances it wouldn't be fair to pin everything on one experience. Perfect or nearly perfect intercourse the first time around may or may not be the case. Mutual adjustments may be needed. If you're sexually incompatible, however, both of you will know soon enough. In any case, the first time should be under the same relaxed circumstances you would have if you were already married or committed to each other. The back seat of a car doesn't provide that. If it's done furtively, or with feelings of guilt, it isn't a fair test.

In its best sense, intercourse isn't something that just comes naturally, as so many people think. For a really satisfactory sexual relationship, techniques have to be learned, and that is where early intercourse can be a help in later life. It's easier to learn when we're young. The important thing is to learn correctly and not fall into some casual pattern that becomes a set way of doing things. If a particular early intercourse experience doesn't lead to marriage or a continuing relationship because of dissatisfaction, it's far better to know it then rather than later. It's still easier to be married than to get unmarried or to end what you thought was a settled relationship.

There's one really bad reason for having early intercourse as an adolescent. Don't do it because "everybody else is doing it." You may think it's a way to maintain status in the group, to be accepted by others, but if that's the only reason or even the most compelling one, intercourse isn't likely to be a satisfying experience. Besides, it's grossly unfair to the girl. You'd simply be using her for your own purposes.

I've given you several good reasons for having intercourse, but it's only sensible to point out the disadvantages. The major one is the danger of pregnancy. Theoretically, the development and availability of contraceptives have removed that danger, but the fact is that not one of these methods is completely safe. I'll have more to say about contraception later, but for now it's enough to note than nothing is 100 percent safe. There is also the possibility of human error in using any of these devices. When people fail to use contraceptives, it's usually because they don't want to admit they're going to have intercourse.

The same thing can be said about sexually transmitted disease. That was once a real possibility until penicillin and other antibiotics were developed. Unfortunately, it's becoming a real possibility again. New strains have developed that are resistant to drugs, and there are now several other venereal diseases to worry about. Overshadowing them all is the menacing threat of AIDS. I'll be talking more about all of these diseases later.

Another problem that may arise out of early adolescent intercourse is to be forced into marriage by pregnancy. While it's true that some people in that situation would have gotten married eventually, it happens more often that a boy and girl who are forced to marry each other will have a much harder time making a good marriage.

Forced marriages aren't nearly as common as they used to be, of course. Abortions have been easier to obtain (until recent Supreme Court decisions), but that's another difficult problem in itself. Another option is to put an unwanted child up for adoption. That can be another kind of emotional complication, not only for young parents at the time but for the adopted child later on.

Then there's an obvious disadvantage in early intercourse, one I've mentioned before—not so much the act itself as where it takes place. If it happens in whatever space is available—a car's rear seat, on a sofa in somebody's house, where discovery might be imminent, or anywhere else it has to be done in a furtive, hurried way, it can be upsetting and probably won't be a really satisfactory experience. Such circumstances ought to be avoided. It doesn't have to be done that way, and it shouldn't be.

Another problem is created when the act is accompanied by a feeling of guilt, and this depends almost entirely on the boy's or the girl's attitude toward what's happening. If you know you're going to feel guilty about it and suffer from attacks of conscience, it's better not to have intercourse at all.

We don't hear so much about it these days, but an attitude from the past that still persists is the fear on the girl's part that a boy will lose respect for her if she permits intercourse. And sometimes that does happen. You can test yourself on this point. Ask yourself how you'd feel about a girl if you knew she had experienced intercourse. Then ask yourself how you'd feel about the special girl you're interested in, the one you want to establish a real relationship with, if you knew she had had intercourse with someone else, maybe even one of your friends. Which would be more important—the relationship you want to have with her, or the fact that she's slept with someone else?

For her part, the girl wants to believe you're more concerned with her as an individual than with what she may have done sexually. If you see her as a sexual object rather than as a girl with a whole personality, you're in trouble. It's the kind of trouble that won't go away when you're older.

Girls have their own ideas about marrying men who have never had intercourse. Even back in the fifties, when Kinsey's study of female sexual behavior was published, less than a quarter of women wanted to marry such a man. A third of them decidedly preferred a man who wasn't a "virgin." About 42 percent didn't care either way. That figure would be much higher today. Unless a jealous personality intervenes, most people no longer care what the other person has done sexually before they got together.

Similarly, guilt feelings about early intercourse that persist into adult life are not much of a problem any more. The more intercourse there is in adolescence, the less the likelihood of guilt later on. Even in the days of the Kinsey Report, only a quarter of married women reported having any regrets, and only 14 percent of those who had had early intercourse over a period of several years expressed regret. I believe both figures would be much lower today. As one might expect, there were fewer regrets among men, but the proportions were about the same. Such regretting must be nearly extinct today.

The overriding fear in adolescent intercourse is that of what happens if you're caught in the act, especially by your parents. Immediate disapproval is virtually certain. There are a good many people also guaranteed to disapprove—teachers, clergy, relatives, the police. Even friends might be disapproving if what you've done violates their own codes or beliefs. Discovery doesn't happen often, but the knowledge that it *can* may spoil the fun. If it *does* happen, embarrassment may be the least of the consequences.

If you and a girl decide you're going to have intercourse, you're probably aware of the risks and don't think of them as any worse than the ones you take every day driving the car on crowded highways. The only way to avoid risks of any kind would be to stay home, where nothing can happen. No one wants to be the kind of person who's so afraid of life that he spends most of his time trying to avoid it. Very few boys fall into that category. So if you've decided to have early intercourse, I'm sure you're well aware of the risks I mentioned earlier, and in the case of possible discovery, won't add to them by doing anything when parents might possibly come home early, let's say, or by having it in a car in some place where a policeman might be shining his flashlight in on you.

There's a more subtle danger in early intercourse. It may result in overemphasizing the physical side of your relationship with a girl. If that's the case, it would be better not to have it. Early sex is better if it's part of the whole relationship between two people. If you're interested only in making out rather than having such a relationship, you may wind up having a good many sexual partners but no female friends. Of course, it's possible for a boy to have a variety of partners yet not let that fact overshadow his relationship with a particular girl.

There are still some adolescents, as well as adults, who think early intercourse without the sanctity of marriage is morally wrong. We've come a long way, though, from the days when we lived by a double standard of morality and men had much more freedom than women. They were expected to "sow their wild oats," and women were supposed to overlook it while at the same time they were considered little better than prostitutes if they did the same thing. Their chances of marrying any "gentleman" were zero. Men's behavior was tolerated because "it's just their nature." Women, on the other hand, were supposed to be pure and undefiled right up to the altar.

Today, of course, all that has virtually disappeared, except for remnants in some parts of society, notably those who follow strict religious beliefs. Girls are now expected to have equal responsibilities and opportunities, in sexual matters as well as in other respects.

In the end, early intercourse in adolescence depends on your own feelings and the feelings of the girl. If either one thinks it's wrong, all the arguments in favor won't make you feel otherwise. And if you and the girl think it *isn't* wrong, all the arguments that might be advanced against it won't make any difference.

For now, let's assume the decision is made, and let's assume further that you're a boy who has never had intercourse with a girl, has never actually examined a girl's sex organs, and isn't too certain he knows as much about the subject as he pretends to.

Some boys are actually surprised to discover that a penis can be inserted into a vagina, because the vaginal opening appears to be little more than a slit. They don't seem to make the connection—or just possibly don't know—that it can accommodate far more than a penis, since babies emerge from it. Think of the vagina as a collapsed balloon that has an astonishing ability to stretch. Inside, it tends to be more or less dry until a girl is aroused sexually. Boys sometimes say a girl in that condition "gets hot," and that's literally true. The walls of the vagina begin to sweat, by a process quite similar to what happens on your face when you exercise. The resulting moisture allows the penis to be inserted more easily. That's why sex play is necessary to make intercourse comfortable.

Before you go any further, however, don't forget to take the necessary precautions that will protect you and the girl from unwanted pregnancy and the danger of AIDS. Put a condom over your penis and be sure it covers the whole length. Current statistics show that these devices fail 30 percent of the time only because they are used improperly, so it's important to remember the rules.

First, use only latex condoms. Keep them in a cool, dry place before using. Don't test them by stretching. Use them, one at a time, *every* time you have intercourse. Open a package carefully so you won't damage the condom with, for example, a long fingernail. Press any air out of a condom at the closed end by pressing your thumb and forefinger at that end. Air bubbles may break condoms. Put a drop of lubricant inside the condom to help it adhere to your skin. Be sure to use a water-based lubricant, not an oil-based lubricant such as baby oil, cold cream, cooking oil, or petroleum jelly, which can eat through the condom. Nonoxynol-9, an ingredient in some lubricants, can kill HIV, the virus that is thought to cause AIDS. Leave about a half inch free at the tip to catch ejaculation.

More precautions. If you're uncircumcised, be sure the foreskin is pulled back before you cover the head. Unroll the condom all the way to the bottom of the penis. It's a good idea to use some lubricant on the outside of the condom and on the girl's vagina before entering. Areas that are too dry may pull off condoms or tear them. Once the penis is inside, be sure the condom isn't slipping, particularly if you get soft. Never leave your penis inside the vagina once you've ejaculated. You can always prevent slippage by holding the base of the condom, and this is also necessary when you withdraw your penis, to prevent spilling any semen. Just withdraw gently and throw the used condom away.

When it comes to penetration of the vagina by the penis, the position taken in the western world is sometimes known as the "missionary" position, in which the girl lies on her back with her legs apart. The boy lies on top of her, face to face, with his legs together. Sometimes the girl helps the boy to insert his penis, although more often he'll do it himself. It's best to make the insertion gradually and slowly, with small thrusts back and forth, rather than in big lunges. A boy can usually tell by the reactions of the female whether he's going too fast for her.

If the girl hasn't had her hymen broken, the breaking that comes with penetration may cause a brief twinge of pain and usually a little bleeding from the torn membrane. There was a time when girls feared all this, thinking of it as a painful experience they had to go through, but both pain and what little blood there is are usually lost in the feelings of the experience itself.

In any case, contrary to popular belief, this doesn't always happen. An unbroken hymen may occasionally be tough and resist the pressure of the penis and cause so much pain and discomfort that a girl does not enjoy the experience on this first try. In rare cases, a doctor has to cut the hymen with an instrument before intercourse can take place. Most often, though, penetration is nearly painless and produces only a few drops of blood.

If a boy encounters any difficulty in breaking the

hymen as he begins to penetrate—and he should do it slowly and carefully if it hasn't been broken—he should take extra care. If the experience is unpleasant for a girl, or if the boy enters her abruptly and without much preparation before she's lubricated and ready for him, it may take her some time to get over it, and she may even feel that sex is distasteful. It's better to have a good deal of fondling and sex play first, with fingers inserted in the vagina, before intercourse takes place for the first time.

Actual intercourse occurs through a series of pelvic thrusts, usually increasing in speed, frequency, and force as the act progresses. Mostly, the boy lies as far forward as possible because that stimulates the area above the vagina, where the clitoris is, and gives the girl more pleasure.

One of the most common problems in intercourse occurs when the male ejaculates too quickly, before the female has a chance to have orgasm. An adolescent boy is likely to do this if he hasn't learned how to delay his orgasm during his masturbatory experiences. He comes rapidly anyway at that age and is usually so eager that he's in a hurry.

There are several things you can do to slow up so the girl will have the longer time it usually takes her to come to orgasm, although that isn't always the case, I might add. Some girls come rapidly, too, and may have several quick orgasms. There's infinite variety in human sexual response. One way a boy can slow himself is to increase the frequency of his ejaculation— that is, ejaculate first by masturbating or through extended sex play, and then go on to intercourse as soon as he's able to have an erection again. It will take him a little longer to get an erection the second time, and probably to ejaculate as well.

Another method is to vary positions. Still another is to do much more prolonged fondling before intercourse even begins, so that the girl will be nearer her climax by the time the boy finally enters her. Or a boy can think about something nonsexual while he's having intercourse (if he's able to) and delay himself. Not everyone can do that.

The "missionary position" was so called because it was assumed in earlier days, when missionaries went abroad to educate "the heathen," that there was only one proper way to have sex. In fact that idea was generally accepted in the western world by many, perhaps most, people in the past, even though nearly every conceivable kind of position had been tried and used since the earliest civilizations. In our time, so much information has been made available, and women today feel so much more freedom in expressing themselves sexually, that both males and females have learned that any one of many positions, or a sequence of several, will provide variety and make the female a more active sexual partner than it was considered proper to be in the past. Women like to do all the things men do, and they're often more inventive.

Let's look at a few of the many positions. In one, the girl lies on top of the boy, with her legs together between his, or vice versa. In this position, it helps if the boy puts his hands on her buttocks, pushing her pelvic area toward his. That will make it easier for her to do her own pelvic thrusts and so build tension for her orgasm. The weight of her body also helps reduce the amount of movement he makes, which again helps him delay ejaculation.

Still another position is for the boy and girl to lie on their sides, facing each other. Often the girl's leg is placed over the boy's leg, allowing them to get closer together. Intercourse can also take place sitting down or standing up. These positions offer variety, but they're not always satisfactory.

In another not uncommon position, the girl's bottom is toward the male as she takes a position on her hands and knees. It's called "dog fashion" since this is the way dogs have intercourse. A girl can also lie on her belly with the boy lying on top of her and entering her vagina from the rear. He's then able to reach under and rub her clitoris, if she likes that. Or she can lie on her side with the boy behind her on *his* side, in which case he is able to stimulate both her clitoris and her breasts after inserting his penis. In yet another position, a boy lies on his back and the girl lies on *her* back on top of him. In all these positions, the clitoris and breasts are made much more accessible for stimulating.

Other cultures have some rather odd ways of intercourse judged by our ways of doing things. For example, in the South Seas, a common method is the Trobriand position, employed by the people who live on those islands, in which the female lies on her back with her legs spread, but instead of lying on her, the male kneels or squats in front of her and makes his pelvic thrusts.

There's no right or wrong way to have intercourse. It's simply a matter of what people want to do and what they think works best for them. Since the world is so full of all kinds of variations in human behavior, we need to remember that what seems strange to us may be commonplace, everyday behavior to someone else. That's true of sexual behavior just as much as eating habits, what we wear, how we speak, and a good many other things. All kinds of factors determine what people do, in sex as much as in anything else. The "missionary position" common in our culture is no more "normal" than what the Trobriand islanders practice. Unfortunately, one of the hardest lessons humans have to learn is how to be tolerant of what others do.

As we've seen, there are differences in male and female behavior during intercourse, and there are also differences between them when it's over. After the male has had his ejaculation, he usually feels relaxed and wants to withdraw his penis at once and go to sleep. But the female wants and appreciates continuing penetration and continuing love play. If you can learn how to go on with this fondling—the same thing you were doing before intercourse—a girl will usually be very appreciative and the experience will be that much more pleasurable for both of you.

If a boy or a girl wants to get out of bed immediately and wash or take a shower, that may reflect an attitude about sex built in since childhood—the feeling that sex is something dirty. A boy should never feel that there's anything unclean about the secretions from his body or hers. Even so, washing after intercourse is at least some precaution against AIDS.

All sorts of sexual pleasure are possible without intercourse, but people have it because once the sexual machine is set in motion, it goes roaring on to its logical conclusion. When people want to get close to each other, intercourse is the closest they can get.

But there are also nonsexual reasons for intercourse, and not all of them are quite so pleasant. One is the feeling of power or authority it gives a male over the female, or sometimes the other way around. Boys have common expressions for this—"I made her," "I laid her," or more explicit equivalents. If you translate these casual boasts, they say, "I imposed my desire, my will, on her." That's why there's sometimes a good deal of hostility in intercourse. Some radical feminists believe it's a hostile act on the part of the male.

There are nonsexual equivalents of this in common speech. People often say, when they've cheated someone in a business transaction, or falsified the worth of an article, or just simply put something over on someone else, "Well, I guess I fucked *him.*" In exactly the same way, a boy can "fuck" a girl instead of having intercourse with her for the positive reasons I've talked about. As we all know, sexual hostility in males can result in forcing a girl to have intercourse against her will. Then it becomes rape, a criminal offense. The law says that girls who are underage (in some states fourteen or younger, in others twenty-one or younger) are incapable of giving consent to intercourse. Having intercourse with an underage girl is called "statutory rape," whether she consents or not. "Criminal rape" occurs when force is used, and it's severely punished by law in every state.

There are girls who engage in intercourse for money, and they're not all prostitutes. Any girl who exchanges her body in return for money or other favors falls into this category. Professional prostitutes work as they always have, either on city streets or out of apartments or hotels, depending on their status. High-priced call girls live in high-priced places and wait for their clients to call them up. At the bottom end of the line, some prostitutes haunt construction sites in cities, or stand on curbs at night and hail passing traffic. Prostitution is as old as humanity, and in spite of today's freedom, it persists, although on a somewhat reduced scale.

There are two major problems with prostitution. One is the very real danger of contracting AIDS. The other is that only sex is involved without affection, friendship, or interchange of feelings, except at the highest levels of the trade. A boy who thinks he's going to learn about sex from a prostitute will be disappointed. All he'll find is a woman who spreads her legs and lets him insert his penis for the shortest possible time. If you've read this far in my book, you'll know there's much more to sex than that.

Prostitutes do have a usual function, although AIDS has made that function a case of Russian roulette. For some men, they provide welcome relief from the sexual frustrations of their lives, and from other anxieties as well. Sex with a prostitute is seldom an act of love, and may often be an expression of real hostility toward women in general, but it's at least a release from tension, even at the minimal level of satisfaction. Not many men would prefer it to sex with someone who wasn't doing it for money. A few men are excited by the element of risk involved—not only the possibility of contracting a disease, but the danger of some criminal act on the part of the prostitute or her pimp, not to mention the risk of doing something illegal.

I hope I've made it clear in this chapter that the most important thing about intercourse is not to have any negative feelings about it. Positive feelings produce the great satisfactions it can give. Even more, I hope you won't see it as the only reason for a relationship with a girl. If it happens, it should be part of a larger relationship based on trust, friendship, responsibility, and respect: the enjoyment of each other's company in other ways besides sex.

CHAPTER · 8

Consequences of the Real Thing

In spite of the fact that many adults seem to have moderated their sexual behavior since the advent of AIDS, a recent survey tells us adolescents have a widespread attitude that they're entitled to have sex. Unlike their parents and grandparents, they feel that they can call the shots—and this feeling applies across the economic and geographic spectrum.

They don't want adults telling them what to do, either. There was a good reason for the success of Madonna's "Papa, Don't Preach." So they feel free to do what they like—until something happens. Then someone else has to come in and pick up the pieces.

I'm sure there isn't a reader of this book who

doesn't know what a condom is, and after reading the previous chapter, he'll know how to use it. Still, there are boys who don't mind playing Russian roulette with their lives. Yet the condom is the most efficient method we have of avoiding pregnancy and AIDS, short of abstinence. According to another survey, teen-agers regard sex as a personal choice, not a rebellion against parents; they respond only to peer pressure. But when things go wrong—pregnancy or sexually transmitted disease—it becomes everybody's business, no matter what our individual views may be.

In the case of pregnancy, another consequence of intercourse may be damaging guilt, although it isn't as common as it used to be. But if a boy cares at all about the girl he's made pregnant, and if her life is now seriously affected by what's happened to her, a boy who cares for other people is likely to feel guilty about the obvious damage he's caused another person. At this point, his peers won't do him much good. It's not their problem. Once the party's over, what happens later is not their concern.

But now parents may come into the picture, and school authorities as well. True, both may be more understanding than they used to be, and girls have more opportunities to get help of some kind in this situation than was once the case, but it's still a messy problem, with all kinds of far-reaching consequences.

Guilt shouldn't be added to these problems. What's required is a sense of responsibility—and honesty. Children are usually taught at a very young age not to lie, that a lie is wrong and the truth is right and there's no in-between. But then they grow up and it begins to be clear that the world is not made up of blacks and whites, but a series of grays.

By the time a boy reaches adolescence, he knows there are times when it's better to lie than to tell the absolute, unsparing truth. These lies are part of every-day social life, and society would be in an extremely uncomfortable situation without them. For example, people tell other people they look fine, or the new dress is pretty, or they can't see you on a particular night because they're ill, or any one of a thousand other "white lies," so that feelings will not be hurt and so that people can live more comfortably together.

People don't feel guilty about telling white lies. What's important is knowing the difference between real dishonesty and the little untruths that enable us to get along in everyday life. You learn to judge situations not by some arbitrary standard of what's right or wrong but on the basis of what makes sense in that particular situation. It's the same way with sex. The difference is that the stakes are much higher and the decisions much harder to make.

I'm not talking here about a boy's decision to start having intercourse at a point when both he and the girl have become so excited that there seems to be no alternative. That's not really a decision. I'm talking about the decision made *before* that happens, when a boy decides he's ready for intercourse, the other boys are calling him a virgin, and he knows a girl who might be willing. At that point, he should understand that if he decides to go ahead, it won't be easy to go back to

his former way of life. For instance, if you have intercourse with a girl, and then decide for one reason or
another that it isn't a good idea to do it with her again,
you won't be able to resume going out with her as you
did before anything happened. Something *has* happened, and it makes a fundamental difference in the
relationship.

For one thing, if you try to go on with the relationship and *don't* have sex with her, even though she may
feel the same way, she'll feel hurt and rejected and the
relationship is likely to end on a bad note. Once a girl
commits herself that much, she is, or believes she is, in
love (unless, of course, she treats sex casually), and
that can be a rocky emotional experience. Once a
course of action is taken, it isn't easy to turn back. At
some time in the past you may have decided to stop
masturbating, but like other boys, you found it impossible.

There isn't much of a halfway point in heavy sex. If
you've gotten to the point of putting your hand on the
girl's sex organ, and then have decided for some reason that you don't want to go that far again, you'll find
it virtually impossible to restrain yourself next time,
unless you're an extremely controlled person. In fact,
the chances are that you'll persist until you've had
intercourse when you go out with her.

I'm sure you see the point here. It's simply that
deciding to have intercourse is a more important decision than others because it commits you to a course of
action that will probably be impossible to reverse if
you want to. Sometimes a girl wants everything *but*

intercourse, and in that case the relationship may survive for a while through mutual fondling until orgasm occurs. There are those who think that this kind of activity is a substitute for masturbation, but it seldom is.

Your grandparents believed—most of them, anyway—that they were somehow obligated to marry if they had intercourse, but few people believe that now. Today it would be unusual for a boy to marry the first girl he has intercourse with. That means a series of relationships with girls that end at various stages of intimacy. A relationship may end with intercourse, and then the boy goes on to a different kind, or the same kind, of relationship with another girl. It's all part of the process of growing up.

Ideally, it would be nice if boys could make these transitions without any harm to themselves or others, but people being what they are, there's bound to be a lot of discomfort along the way. Adolescent love affairs are more often unhappy than not, regardless of whether they go as far as intercourse. But somehow both boys and girls survive.

I'm not suggesting that the best way to grow into adulthood is to go from one sex experience to another with a great number of girls. What I *do* say is that if you develop a variety of sexual and social experiences with something more involved in them than sex, the transition from adolescence will be easier. Some boys discover that even sex can be boring if it isn't combined with some real emotion between the two people involved—affection, mutual caring, friendship. And once this complete kind of relationship has been experienced, everything else will seem unsatisfactory.

Getting back now to the consequences of intercourse, pregnancy is not necessarily one of them. Most boys understand how it can be avoided through the different methods that come under the heading of contraception. Some methods are better than others, but there isn't one that's guaranteed.

Withdrawal is probably the most commonly used method, particularly by young people, or at least those who don't have the money, opportunity, or motivation to practice mechanical means. Withdrawal before ejaculation sounds simple and easy, and of course it doesn't require any apparatus, but unfortunately it isn't as simple as it sounds.

In the first place, it isn't as enjoyable, because at the height of sexual excitement, when both people are most involved with the act, the boy's whole desire is to push in, but it's just at that moment that he must pull out. His excitement may be so great that he won't be able to stop, but even if he does, there may be enough sperm in the lubricating fluid that comes out of his penis before he ejaculates to make a girl pregnant. It's also possible for a male to ejaculate at the opening of the vagina, and even though the girl may still have her hymen intact, sperm can find their way through it and move all the way up the length of the vagina into the uterus. So withdrawal isn't only unsatisfactory, it's also unsafe.

Another method is to avoid having intercourse when the egg is in the process of coming out of the ovary and down into the Fallopian tubes. If we could be absolutely sure when that was happening, pregnancy could be avoided successfully by not having intercourse during the few hours of the month when this process occurs. But the problem is, how to be sure. If a girl keeps an accurate record of her menstrual periods, the process may be pinpointed at fourteen days before she begins the next menstruation. That will be accurate, however, only if she has regular periods, which many girls do not, and if she ovulates only once a month. Some girls ovulate more often than that.

Obviously, this kind of contraception—sometimes known as the rhythm method—is far from safe. Nevertheless, it's the only one approved by the Catholic Church. At best, however, it's a halfhearted method of contraception, and too often not successful.

The most common kind of contraception is the condom, a method that's centuries old. Before rubber was invented, silk handkerchiefs or other fabrics were used, but they were not very reliable. Now we have a variety of rubber sheaths to fit over the penis, some of them prelubricated, that will catch the semen and prevent the sperm from going up into the uterus. Since the AIDS epidemic began, condoms have been made available on a scale never seen before. Only fifty years ago they were often sold under the counter in drugstores. Now anyone can buy them, no questions asked. (I've discussed how to use them in a previous chapter.) Taking everything into account, condoms are the best contraceptive device available—about 99 percent effective.

This claim may be challenged by those who favor what we familiarly call "the pill." Contraceptive pills have been in use long enough now to evaluate, but still they're the subject of medical controversy. They have been refined, but some doctors believe they may have serious long-range effects, and sometimes the well-known short-range effects—weight gain, occasional nausea—that are seen in some women are undesirable. To be effective, the pills must be taken, one a day, for twenty-one days, and then stopped in order to menstruate. That creates a hazard of its own, if a girl forgets a day or two, or takes them irregularly. As for the side effects, doctors who must prescribe the pills usually keep track of their patients to see what the side effects, if any, may be. Nothing has been firmly established about the long-range effects. Any girl who fears taking the pill for any reason shouldn't do it. The anxiety about intercourse wouldn't be worth it.

Another factor in using the pill is that few girls an adolescent boy is likely to go out with will be using it. It may require a doctor's prescription, which means parents may know, and not many of them are likely to approve if the girl is very young.

But aside from the condom, the pill is the best method of contraception we have until something better comes along. Girls who use it properly don't have to worry about getting pregnant. If it fails, it's nearly always the result of carelessness.

There are other methods of contraception, but

they all have their drawbacks. One is for the girl to wash out her vagina with water containing some antiseptic after intercourse. This is known as a douche (pronounced *doosh*). It requires a douche bag, an apparatus that looks like a hot-water bottle with a tube; it forces water into the vagina. It's most unlikely that any girl will carry one of these devices with her when she goes out with a boy, and she won't have one at home unless she uses it for hygienic purposes.

This fact has led to some unusual substitutes. Some adolescents think that if you take a cola bottle and shake it up, then squirt it into the vagina by placing the thumb partly over the top, you'll be able to flush out sperm after intercourse. No one knows how many pregnancies this erroneous belief has caused. But no matter whether it's a carbonated beverage or water, the douche is a very poor and ineffective method of contraception. It's even dangerous if antiseptics are used. Some of them can burn or irritate the vagina.

Still another contraceptive device, one much more common among adult women than young girls until recently, is a dome-shaped vaginal cap made of rubber, known as a diaphragm. It must be fitted by a doctor, since it comes in different sizes to accommodate the varying sizes of women. This cap fits over the cervix and closes off the entrance to the uterus so the sperm can't enter. Not only must it be fitted by a doctor to be sure the size is right, but the woman must learn how to put it in herself, using a special cream or jelly with it, before intercourse. It must be left in for eight hours afterward. Again, this isn't a method young girls are very likely to be using, and some adult women don't like it for various reasons. Moreover, doctors may not want to fit a girl unless her parents consent. Some physicians draw the line at a particular age if they think parental approval is required.

Women also use foams, jellies, creams, suppositories, or tablets instead of the diaphragm, but none of these has proved to be as safe as the condom. For aesthetic reasons, most girls don't want to use them, in any case.

There is also the intrauterine device, commonly known as the IUD, made of plastic, which comes in several shapes and is inserted into the uterus by a doctor and left there for months or even years. When it was first introduced, many doctors thought the IUD was ideal, since it was easy to insert and was virtually guaranteed to prevent pregnancy. But drawbacks appeared. First, it was found that it couldn't be used effectively by women who had never had a child. Then, more recently, questions were raised about its safety, including the possibility that it might cause uterine cancer. There isn't much enthusiasm for the IUD these days.

Whatever the means, it's important to remember that contraception can be the responsibility of either the male or the female. Today, for the first time, mostly as the result of AIDS, girls and women, as well as boys and men, may carry condoms and insist that they be used. Other than that, males have only withdrawal as a possible technique until a pill is invented for *them,* which may not be far off, and in fact is here experimentally. All other contraceptive methods are for females to use. The condom places considerable responsibility on the male, although today females are taking it, too. Adolescent boys need to remember that there's no such thing as being a little pregnant, and if they decide to take a chance, they had better be prepared for the possible consequences.

What should a boy do if he *does* make a girl pregnant? The girl herself has four options. She can get married, or at least start living with the boy, if circumstances permit and if that's their mutual decision. Often it's the worst choice, because both are likely to be too young to start family life. Usually a boy can't support a wife at that stage, and schooling for both of them would be interrupted. Marriages that begin because people "have to get married" are usually not as successful as those that happen because both people want it.

A second option is for the girl to have the baby and keep it, or else put it up for adoption. If she decides to keep it, the problem is how to support herself and the child, a responsibility that parents usually have to take on. Taking this course can, and probably will, change a girl's life completely—often in ways she would never have wanted. Adoption is not an easy matter, either. First there is the emotional shock of giving up the baby with the prospect of never seeing it again, something not every girl is able to do. It may not be fair to the child, either. Adopted children often have problems of their own when they are told what happened to them.

A fourth option is abortion, currently one of the most controversial issues in American life, with fierce opinions on both sides and much else involved besides the fact of the abortion itself. Abortion was not legal under any circumstances until the famous *Roe v. Wade* decision of 1973 by the United States Supreme Court, which permitted it with three qualifications. (See Chapter 10, question 4). Before this happened, abortions occurred anyway, often by unqualified doctors under squalid circumstances. Today an abortion is relatively easy to obtain, from thoroughly qualified doctors under the best conditions.

In 1989, however, the abortion situation was complicated by a new Supreme Court decision. In a revisionary ruling, *Webster v. Reproductive Health Services,* a Missouri law was upheld that sharply restricts abortion and requires doctors to test for the viability of a fetus at twenty weeks. Whether there will be further restrictions as the result of pending cases, in effect possibly overturning *Roe v. Wade* and making abortion illegal once more, remains to be seen as we go to press.

If you read the papers, you know that the "Right to Life" movement in the United States, religiously inspired, is carrying on a crusade to have the Supreme Court's decision reversed. If this is successful, what I'm saying here will be academic. But for now, let's assume that it will stand. That doesn't mean the issue will go away, because if you make a girl pregnant and you're confronted with the choice, you and she—most particularly, she—will have to make the decision according to your beliefs about abortion, whether they're religious or not. So what I am giving you here is simply information you need to know if the decision is in favor of abortion.

When the operation is done correctly, by a qualified physician in an office or hospital, it is safer than a tonsillectomy. It can be dangerous only in the hands of incompetent doctors or of abortionists who are not even doctors and who work under unsterile conditions. In those circumstances, infection or death can result. Infection may mean that a girl will not be able to get pregnant ever again.

When a boy makes a girl pregnant, he's likely to be depressed and anxious, even terrified, by the situation he finds himself in, and ignorant of where to turn for help. The first thing he needs to do is to be sure that the girl is actually pregnant. This is done by a medical test, using either a blood sample or a sample of the girl's urine. The test is done in a laboratory, following a visit to a doctor. There is also a simple test that can be bought over the counter at a drugstore.

If the pregnancy is confirmed, guilt and fear are likely to set in. The last people a boy may want to know about it are his parents, yet in most cases it's the parents he should turn to first for help. That may be difficult to do, but it's often the best course of action because the alternatives may be even more difficult. A boy may be surprised to discover the support he'll get from his parents in such circumstances. It's true, however, that there are others who will react only with anger; it won't be much consolation for them to realize they've failed the test of being good parents.

The reaction of the girl's parents will be about the same in general, although they will think their problem is worse, and probably they'll blame the boy for the whole thing, even though he and the girl may have shared responsibility.

But if, for some reason, you can't turn to your parents, there are other sources of help—people like the family doctor, a minister, a priest, a rabbi, a teacher or a counselor at school you can trust, or possibly an aunt or an uncle you feel close to.

First, however, you should talk things over with the girl before *anything* is done. Then she should discuss the problem with the people *she* trusts, whoever they are, so that a decision about what to do can be reached as soon as possible. Time is important, if abortion is to be the option. If it is, the girl's family (or whoever she has taken into her confidence) will probably make the arrangements. It should be done before the end of the third month. After that, the fetus is large enough to make the operation possibly dangerous, and many doctors will not perform it.

Before the decision is made, there are a few false ideas to avoid. Pay no attention to anyone who suggests some drug that will cause a miscarriage—that is, loosen the fetus from its position on the uterine wall so it will fall down into the vagina and out of the body. Quinine, castor oil, ergot, and other drugs are commonly thought to cause miscarriages. They almost never work, and when they do, it's only in cases where the girl would have had a miscarriage anyway at some point in her pregnancy. It's true that a small percentage of pregnancies (perhaps one in twenty) will end in miscarriage anyway, but obviously these are not very good odds when it comes to ending an unwanted pregnancy.

Girls, in a state of desperation, have been known to try to induce abortion: A girl may fall on her abdomen, insert something into the uterus (the coathanger was a common device in prelegalization days), jump down from a high place, or jar her body in some other way. These are very dangerous practices, possibly leading to injury, infection, or even death. Fortunately, most girls today know too much about sexual matters to make any such attempt.

Now, with all these facts in mind, let's go back to the moment of fertilization. If that moment can be prevented, all the options I've described here will not be necessary. I think the lesson is clear.

But there's another possible consequence of intercourse besides pregnancy, and that's the possibility of contracting a sexually transmitted disease. Such transmissions result only from some form of sexual contact, and that danger is always present. AIDS is at the top of the list these days because, unlike the others, it is almost always fatal and, as of 1990, there is no known cure. Until this virus appeared, the two most common sexually transmitted diseases for centuries were syphilis and gonorrhea. Since they're more common, let's talk about them first.

In gonorrhea, the first symptom for a boy is a burning in the penis when he urinates. This symptom develops from eight to fifteen days after intercourse with a girl who's infected. However, you won't contract gonorrhea from an infected girl every time you have intercourse with one, anymore than you catch a cold every time you're exposed to someone who's sniffling and sneezing.

The germs that cause gonorrhea, known as gonococci, enter the opening of the penis and multiply in the urethra. This results in the burning sensation that is the first symptom. Shortly afterward, pus with a characteristic and rather unpleasant odor begins to drip from the penis. Any boy who has these symptoms should get to a doctor as soon as possible. If it's the family doctor, there's always the fear that he or she will tell the parents. That may be true of some doctors, but others will respect the confidential nature of the relationship between a doctor and a patient in these cases as they would in any other.

But the doctor *is* required by law to report the case to the local board of health. Some do, some don't; there are undoubtedly a great many unreported cases. If it's reported, the board of health will want to know where the boy got the disease (or the girl, of course). They will ask what girls he had intercourse with and will want to examine them to see which one is infected. That's likely to be embarrassing, but it's absolutely essential if we're ever going to lower the VD rate.

Boards of health are not interested in condemning a boy or exposing him. They want only to track down the source of infection. Consequently, if a boy's physician reports the case, his identity will be protected, and so will a girl's.

The old forms of venereal disease aren't the scourge they used to be. Gonorrhea once could be cured only by long and sometimes painful treatment, if it was cured at all. Syphilis ran rampant through the world, unchecked for centuries, and even in this century it was still known as "the great killer" and also "the great imitator." The discovery of penicillin and the sulfa drugs has brought these diseases more or less under control—"less" because recently strains resistant to drugs have been appearing and we may have to revise our approach.

In any case, it's important not to treat such sexually transmitted diseases lightly. Don't listen to anyone who tells you, "It's no worse than a bad cold." Without treatment, the consequences are far worse than a bad cold, and in the case of syphilis, they can even be fatal.

If you have any symptoms of gonorrhea, then, go to the doctor immediately. Penicillin shots are the preferred treatment, and 95 percent of cases clear up after one to three shots. If they don't, sulfa drugs are employed. But immediate treatment is important. If gonorrhea is not treated, the burning sensation and the dripping will stop, probably leading the victim to think the disease has cured itself. But the germ will still be active in his body, and it may have serious consequences later.

Unlike gonorrhea, the syphilis germ can invade the body through any mucous membrane. You can get gonorrhea only by putting your penis into the vagina of an infected girl. Syphilis, however, can be absorbed not only through the end of the penis or from the vagina, but also from the other person's mouth, either in kissing or oral intercourse, although it's rare to get the disease in other ways than through intercourse. The germ lives for only about three seconds outside a moist environment, so it's ridiculous to believe, as some do, that you can get it by sitting on a toilet seat.

The first symptom of syphilis is usually a single sore that is not painful and is followed by a rash that may appear on almost any part of the body. This rash can be so light and last for so short a time that you might not notice it. That symptom appears anywhere from ten to ninety days after infection. The sore, called a chancre, may occur on the penis or in the vagina or, in rare cases, at some point where the syphilis germ was able to invade through a break in the skin. The chancre appears about sixty days after infection. It will go away in time, but if there is no treatment, the disease stays with the person, sometimes seeming to disappear and not reappearing until months or even years later. When it comes again, it will be in a later and much more virulent state, and then it can do serious damage to the organs of the body and may result in death.

Penicillin shots are also the treatment for syphilis. The series of shots lasts for about five days and is almost always effective. As I've said, both syphilis and gonorrhea can be extremely serious diseases if they're not treated, and that's particularly true of syphilis. We're fortunate in having a cure for them that's quick and simple—up to this point, at least. The resistant strains may be a more serious problem.

You may want to know if the symptoms of gonorrhea and syphilis are the same for girls. By and large they are, except that the girl's sex organs are more hidden, so it's more difficult to spot the symptoms. With gonorrhea, she will have a painful irritation in the lining of the urethra, which will produce pus. But since this secretion will not be so easily noticed as in the boy, a girl may think it's nothing more than a vaginal infection of some kind.

In syphilis, the girl will develop the same characteristic chancre, but it can be hidden in the vagina or mouth so that she (and the boy) never know she has it. There's a common superstition that you can tell whether a girl has a sexually transmitted disease by pouring whiskey or even a carbonated soft drink on her sex organ, and if it burns, she's infected. There's no truth in this idea. Unless a girl has a visible chancre on the lips of the vagina or notices a discharge of pus from the urethra, she won't be able to tell whether she has such a disease or not.

There are other less well known diseases in this category that are not life threatening but extremely uncomfortable and possibly disabling. One is NGU, or nongonococcal urethritis. It is now the most common sexually transmitted disease. It was thought to be no more than a minor problem until recently, when it was discovered that it could cause lifelong sterility in men and women if not treated. Some specialists believe that one variety of NGU bacteria is possibly more dangerous than gonococcus.

Since most women don't have symptoms of NGU and so become carriers without knowing it, and since cases aren't usually reported to health officials, it has spread rapidly until it affects more than two million people a year. While it doesn't usually respond to penicillin, other antibiotics are effective. You should see your doctor if you notice any pain or secretions of pus in your genital area or in urination.

Still another venereal disease that isn't as well known as the others—or at least it wasn't until recently —is an invasion by the germs called herpes simplex— the same ones that cause cold sores. They can spread through sexual contact and the result is an extremely painful infection of the genitals in both men and women. It isn't fatal, or damaging to organs, but the pain and irritation are enough to put those who have it out of the running sexually for some time, and it's a very unpleasant disease to endure. Worse, there's no cure as yet, only medication to ease the pain and itching. It goes away in time, but it may recur again and again, at different intervals, indefinitely. Anyone who has these symptoms should simply stop having sex until they recede.

Overshadowing all the diseases I've been talking about, however, is the great plague of our century, AIDS. You may have been getting some AIDS education at your school, or from some other source—newspapers and magazines have been full of information— but in case you haven't, here are the facts.

AIDS means Acquired Immune-Deficiency Syndrome. It is thought to be caused by HIV—the human immunodeficiency virus, which destroys the body's natural immune system. As of 1990, there is no known cure and therefore AIDS must be presumed to be fatal, sooner or later. As the immune system breaks down, patients are made vulnerable to all kinds of infections, tumors, neurological disorders, and other diseases. Often the breakdown takes the form of a very dangerous lung infection, or a form of skin cancer, or both. The skin cancer once affected mostly elderly men and was slow acting, but in AIDS patients it is rapid and devastating. AIDS is a worldwide disease, possibly originating in Africa, where there are great numbers of cases in both men and women.

Scientists and researchers are still learning about AIDS. They believe that being infected by the virus is not in itself enough to cause AIDS, but other factors have to be present—another virus, perhaps, or a previous weakening of the immune system. Numerous other questions await answers. It isn't clear, for example, how many of those infected with the virus will actually develop AIDS, and if they do, when it will happen. It's likely, but not certain, that they will be infectious to others throughout their lives, even if they never develop the disease. It may also be true that some people develop light or severe symptoms after an amount of time that no one can pinpoint, but may never actually have what can be unmistakably identified as AIDS. No statistics are available, but there may be as many as ten times the number of such cases as those who have AIDS, and the number of infected people with no symptoms at all is a hundred times higher than those with the "mild" cases.

It's incorrect to say that you "catch" AIDS. You may be infected by the HIV virus, and over a period of time you may or may not wind up having AIDS.

You can get this virus only by very intimate physical contact and the exchange of bodily fluids. It has been isolated in blood, semen, vaginal secretions, mother's milk, saliva, urine, feces, even tears. Most experts agree, however, that transmission is possible only through the exchange of blood, semen, or vaginal secretions because the concentration of the virus in the other sources would require exchanging an inordinate amount of fluid. Many authorities believe there are factors in saliva that kill HIV.

HIV infection can be acquired through blood transfusions, through the sharing of unsterilized needles among drug users, or if infected blood from an open wound comes into contact with an abrasion, break, or cut in another person's skin. Most of the time, however, infection occurs during intimate sexual contact, when several of these fluids pass from one body to another. Infected semen, for example, may enter the body through oral, vaginal, or anal intercourse. It isn't certain yet whether the exchange of saliva in deep kissing can transmit the virus by itself, but it seems quite possible if one person is infected and the other, for instance, has bleeding gums. This kind of transmission is hard to prove, however, because people who deep-kiss are likely to be having other kinds of intimate contact as well.

In our anxiety about the spread of AIDS, we're inclined to forget that it's not transmitted easily, and that it can't be transmitted through casual social contact. The virus can't be sent through the air, and you can't get it by shaking hands with an infected person, or even by hugging and dry kissing. Nor can you get it by sharing a workplace or a schoolroom or a household with an infected person. Of course, it would be safer not to share things like razor blades.

There are two major behaviors that put you at risk: sexual intercourse and sharing needles among intravenous drug users.

Does that mean you have to stop having sex? Not at all. But if you have sexual contact with someone, you should assume, for the sake of safety and to protect your life, that the other person may be carrying the AIDS virus, even though your partner may have no idea that she (or he) does. This means you should avoid any risky behavior and take the precautions I've discussed earlier to avoid both disease and unwanted pregnancy. You should do this even though it's true that most people are not at risk. Anything that prevents the exchange of fluids is the front line of defense, and using spermicides will make things even safer. If they're sexually active, both boys and girls should carry condoms lubricated with nonoxynol-9 and know how to use them. Boys need to remember that they could be infected by either boys or girls, and using condoms will protect both.

Never have sex when you're drunk or high. That's the time you don't take precautions, and it could be your last chance to take them. Anyway, sex is its own high. Drug users should never share intravenous-drug needles, and no one should have unprotected sex with anyone who has ever shared these needles. No matter how much you want to have sex, and how urgent the opportunity may be, remember that none of this is worth risking unprotected intercourse. Dying from AIDS is one of the worst ways to go. And don't let yourself be talked into sex for nonsexual reasons. Don't depend on the other person to provide the protection or the good judgment required in sexual situations. Don't give in to being begged or threatened.

I hope all these dos and don'ts won't frighten boys into a life of celibacy, although that isn't very likely, I know. It's simply a matter of recognizing a great danger and being sensible about it. People have a right to sex, but they also have a responsibility, and never more so than in the case of AIDS.

If you're ready for sexual intercourse, and are able to have it, the important thing is, first of all, to be safe and secure wherever you're having it, in an atmosphere free of anxiety. Casual sex is not a good idea in any case, but AIDS and the other sexually transmitted diseases make it a danger as well. The condom is the best protection you can have—that and the exercise of your good common sense. Then sex can be the exciting, rewarding experience it should always be.

You should also consider that satisfactory sex is possible without penetrating the vagina, thus avoiding the possibility of either AIDS or pregnancy. A couple may caress and stroke each other and follow this by masturbating each other. In this case, however, to be absolutely safe, nonoxynol-9 should be applied to the fingers beforehand, and the hands should be washed afterward. It can also be satisfying if both you and your partner masturbate yourselves while lying together and caressing each other. While you're avoiding AIDS and pregnancy, you can also be discovering things about your personal sexuality you didn't know before.

CHAPTER · 9

What Being Gay Is All About

Loving other people is one of the most important things we do. Everybody needs to love and be loved. Without loving and caring, it would be hard to sustain life in any satisfactory way. Most people love someone of the opposite sex and hope to be loved in return. But there are those who find that they love a person of the same sex. It may be only a passing experience for some, but for others—perhaps one in ten—it is a life pattern. Some people simply prefer to have sex with those of their own sex, whatever their feelings may be for them.

It's these relationships we call homosexuality, but it would be a mistake to lump them all together under one name. Dr. Kinsey graded sexual behaviors on a scale of zero to six. At the upper end were those who were totally involved with the same sex and never intended to have relations with anyone of the other sex. These were rated at six. They were simply not aroused by females. At the zero end of the scale were those who had never experienced homosexual contact and did not believe they ever would.

Most people lie somewhere in between on Kinsey's scale. Many studies have shown that a high percentage of boys have some kind of homosexual contact while they're growing up but never repeat it in adult life. Others do repeat the experience if the occasion offers. Still others, in the middle of the scale, are bisexual; they enjoy sexual relations with either sex. Approaching the six, or high, end of the scale, there are those who prefer the same sex in increasing degrees, to the final point of total commitment.

It's important to learn to love, no matter what the sex of the loved one may be. That's much of what life is all about. People who happen to love someone of the same sex are having the same kind of necessary experience as those who love in a heterosexual way.

Today there is much more acceptance of homosexuality in society than ever before. Homosexuals call themselves "gay," so that in addition to its old meaning (happy and lighthearted), the word now designates anyone who acknowledges his, or her, homosexuality. Gays have organized to defend their rights as human beings and as citizens. "Gay pride" is the common slogan, and with this goes "gay rights." Gay men and women unite in this movement, since there are few differences between the sexes in this matter. As a result of pressure, old laws have been changed in some places to lessen the discrimination against gays, but the struggle is far from over.

About half the states still have laws prohibiting homosexual behavior, and in some of them the penalties are severe. A few of these laws go back to the nation's early days. Even Thomas Jefferson supported a law that prescribed castration for homosexuals. Most religious faiths condemn homosexuality—certainly all the major ones do—and large sections of the population still join in the condemnation.

What is against the law everywhere is for grown men to have sex with boys. In many states boys who have sex with each other can be prosecuted as juvenile delinquents and sent to institutions. Fortunately it's virtually impossible to enforce such laws; otherwise, there would not be enough jails to hold all the offenders.

Our greater acceptance of homosexuality today has led some people to believe there has been a rise in the number of gays, but there is no real evidence to prove it. We *think* there are more because so many are now able to acknowledge their preference—to "come out," as the phrase goes. Since so many have become political activists, homosexuals are highly visible. Citizens who may never knowingly have associated with a gay person now see them on their television screens playing public and positive roles, and read of their achievements in many occupations.

More people, too, now understand that homosexual men are not necessarily effeminate—in fact, those who are constitute a minority. Some are professional football players, or are rugged-looking individuals in the entertainment or other businesses. People who think that they can always identify a gay person are mistaken.

With the greater sexual freedom we enjoy today, permitting more experimentation, some people have discovered they enjoy relations with both sexes. In doing this, they are only following what we learn as children. Sexually, children act very much like other mammals. All religions believe that what separates men and women from their fellow mammals is their souls, and that is a matter of faith. But massive scientific evidence also shows many similarities in sexual behavior between people and animals.

All mammals, for instance, have in common the characteristic of self-play with the penis. In chimpanzees, the usual method is to put their mouths on their own penises, which, as I noted earlier, many boys try and almost always fail to do. Another common characteristic is that all mammals perform intercourse by the male's thrusting the pelvis forward and backward, even though in most animals the female is backed up against the male.

Similarly, all species of mammals have homosexual relations. Boys who live on farms, or who have visited them, have seen cows mounting other cows. Perhaps they've seen the same thing happen at the zoo, where such behavior is often observed among monkeys and apes.

Since we're all mammals, then, it's reasonable to wonder why all boys don't engage in homosexual behavior. They don't, of course, and I'm not suggesting they should. Boys soon learn that there are conflicts about homosexuality in the society they live in, and if they thought about it, they'd see that the conflicts arise because people have a tendency to put everything into compartments. They want to classify everything as extremes or opposites.

In America, for example, we've always had the "good guys" and the "bad guys"—cowboys and Indians, cops and robbers, and so on. In real life, though, often it turns out that the good guys aren't all good, and the bad guys not all bad. Extremes exist, but most of us are more gray than black and white, just as most people are neither short nor tall but somewhere in between.

Boys aren't necessarily either "gay" or "straight," either. If a boy finds himself involved in some kind of sex play with boys while he's growing up, as many do, that doesn't mean he isn't interested in girls, or is much more interested in boys. Nor does it mean that these boys can't or won't have intercourse with girls and eventually get married. Homosexuality is much more a state of mind than it is actual behavior. It's simply a matter of sexual preference. And the same thing can be said of the straight ones, the heterosexuals.

Some boys never have any homosexual experiences and are never aroused by other males. And then there are those at the other extreme, and the great majority in between. But it isn't that simple. Many boys are aroused by or have physical contact with both boys and girls, ranging from the boy who has had sex only once with another male and has had a lot of sex with girls, to the boy who has had sex only once with a girl but has had a lot of sex with boys. Only a relative few have had a fair amount of sex with both boys and girls.

Freud thought homosexuality was no more than a phase of sexual development. He believed humans moved from an early narcissism (a preoccupation with self) to homosexuality, and then to heterosexuality. Many of his followers came to believe that if an individual didn't go through these stages, there was something wrong with him. That led for a time to such absurd practices as encouraging homosexual behavior among boys in their early teens so that they would progress safely into heterosexuality. I don't believe in this theory. In all the thousands of boys and men I've talked to about their sex lives, I've seen this progression very infrequently. I believe boys have sex with other boys for a variety of reasons, some positive and some negative.

Why does it happen? Because, for instance, a boy may be afraid of girls, and be so timid and shy he can't join them socially. Consequently, if he's going to have any sex at all, aside from masturbation, it will have to be with boys. There are others who don't want to have sex with girls because of a hatred for them, real or imaginary. This may have arisen from a bad experience with a girl in which the boy's pride was badly hurt, so that he was deprived of his self-confidence and he reacted with hostility and anger.

Sometimes, too, boys get started in sex with other boys for no better reason than because it's the easiest thing to do, and boys are much more available. If a boy asks his mother whether Jimmy can come over and spend the night, she'll most likely be pleased he has company and make no objection. Staying overnight, for both boys and girls, is such a common practice that parents don't give it any thought. But imagine what the same mother would say if her son asked to have his friend Mary spend the night!

Boys see a lot of each other—in gym classes, on hikes, in the clubhouse, in swimming, and in a hundred other activities. They are often alone with other boys when they're undressed, and that's an opportunity they don't have with girls. Obviously, boys are much more easily available for sex experiences.

Without being told, a boy knows that what pleases him must be pleasing to other boys. When he masturbates, for instance, it's easy for him to transfer the knowledge of this pleasure to another boy, but much harder for him to understand a girl's feelings. He also has much more in common to talk about with other boys, like things they're both interested in doing.

If it's all so easy and pleasurable, then, why shouldn't boys have unlimited sex play with each other? There are two reasons why it may not be such a good thing. First, society disapproves of this behavior, and a boy runs the risk of being censured or punished, perhaps severely, if he's discovered. Secondly, he may find these contacts so pleasurable that he won't give himself the chance to find out about heterosexual life, which might please him a great deal more.

Boys often get interested in other boys in the process of building up their bodies in our fitness-conscious society. Many young boys work out with barbells and other exercisers to get in good condition for sports or simply to have fit bodies. Boys have always been intrigued, particularly if they have inferior physiques, by ads that promise to develop them into strongmen, and our society today encourages this kind of thing more than ever before. Boys get the idea that if they're not musclemen, girls won't be attracted to them—and for some girls, at least, that's true. This —their natural inclination to athletics—makes many boys more than willing to exercise or go out for sports.

No one complains about this. No one objects to boys being strong and muscular and healthy. The problem is that some get so interested in their own bodies, so preoccupied with building themselves up, that in time they don't think of much else. Inevitably, they compare their bodies with those of other boys, admiring and envying those with better physiques. Sometimes this admiration takes the form of being sexually aroused by the others, and out of this comes the desire to have sex with the body of another person of the same sex.

There's a common misconception about homosexuality that "some boys are born queer." No study has produced any solid evidence that this is true, but the researchers still aren't absolutely sure. When an individual is born, he has the ability to do anything sexually. *What* he does depends on what experiences he has. So it's safe to say that if he isn't born homosexual, he isn't born heterosexual, either. He's simply born as a sexual person.

Another popular belief is that homosexuals have different kinds of glands. There is absolutely no evidence to support this idea. Nevertheless, some people think male homosexuals have special glands in their throats that make them want oral contact with a man's penis. That isn't true, either. Comparisons of body builds of homosexuals with heterosexuals show no anatomical differences between them.

We're all familiar with boys who are overly attached to their mothers—"mama's boys," we say. That sometimes turns out to be unfortunate because a boy in that situation may not grow up to be an independent human being. On the other hand, it doesn't mean he's a homosexual, as some people think. In reality, many "mama's boys" are definitely not homosexual and many males who *are* homosexual are *not* "mama's boys."

A mother whose overprotection keeps a boy from playing with other boys or participating in rough games won't necessarily make her son a homosexual, but there is always the possibility that it might. If a boy is excluded from the gang, it's bound to be hurtful. Hoping to be accepted may make him want to imitate the boys who *are* accepted, which sometimes creates a sexual interest in another boy.

There are relatively few boys who like to dress up like girls, a practice known as "transvestism," or cross dressing. Boys who like to do this often get started in the practice as early as four or five, frequently in the common game of "playing house." Sometimes a boy does this because he wants to get some sort of acceptance or affection from an older sister or a playmate while he's dressed as a girl. At that point a connection is made in his mind between that acceptance or affection and what he's doing, and this may carry over into adult life.

Whether transvestism begins with playing house, or dressing up for Halloween, or in some other way, sexual interest may become fixed in this practice because the boy gets an unusual amount of attention, more than he'd get otherwise. The attention may or may not be favorable, but at least he's noticed, and if he needs attention badly, he'll continue to do whatever will attract it.

It's a curious fact that even though they like to dress as girls, transvestites are usually heterosexual. They don't want to *be* girls, they just want to dress like them. If they concentrate their interest in girls' clothing on specific articles, things like panties, stockings, or brassieres, they're called fetishists. A fetishist is aroused sexually by something that is not part of the female body but is associated with it in his mind.

Some boys, however, not only want to dress like girls, they want to *be* girls. They're called "transsexuals," and the reason they want to dress like girls is that on some level they believe they *are* girls. This kind of behavior also starts very early in life, even earlier than transvestism. As these boys begin to grow up, they think of all the things in a girl's life they'd like for themselves—things like not being roughed up, or wearing pretty clothes, or doing the things girls do together. They don't think boys have any advantages. Transsexuals are usually homosexual. But because they think of themselves as females, they believe they're heterosexual. A few have operations that change them from males to females, as far as it's possible. After the operation, some transsexuals even legally marry males—and indeed, after a sex-change operation, they *are* females.

On the other side of the coin, there are also female transsexuals who want to become males and have operations designed to accomplish it. The chances for any realistic success, however, are not as great in this case. No one knows how many transvestites and transsexuals there are in the male—or the female—population, but there's reason to believe there are more than people think—perhaps one in every two hundred males.

If you wonder why I'm taking so much space to talk about these variations from what we think of as "normal," it's because I hope boys who read this will understand what the variations are and how they happen, so that they will develop tolerance for people who may not be like them. A mature boy is one who can accept these differences as a fact of life and who won't bully a "sissy" or sneer at homosexuals and try to put them down in one way or another.

In 1949 there was a movie called *The Boy with Green Hair,* which was about, as you might expect, a boy who happened to have been born with green hair. It was a fantasy, of course, because that's not a biological possibility. Like all human beings, this boy needed love and acceptance in his own group, but all he got was antagonism, even hatred, because he wasn't like the others.

This is the kind of intolerance that has caused a great deal of human misery in the world. I hope the boys who read this book, and through it come to understand the real nature of the sexual world we live in, will be tolerant of those who aren't like themselves. Remember, those others *are* like you in most other ways. They just happen to have "green hair."

The generation growing up now in an atmosphere of much greater sexual freedom seems to be much more tolerant of others than their parents were, although no one should be overly optimistic about that. But generation by generation, we appear to be moving slowly in this direction. Most parents, however, still think of homosexuality with distaste, even hatred, and regard it as dangerous and a threat to their children. To many the object is so abhorrent that they won't talk about it except to condemn it. In the arts, however, progress has been made. Moviemakers, who for so long never treated homosexuality on the screen with anything but derision, now have made sensitive pictures on the subject, and excellent plays continue to be written about it. Homosexuality is commonplace in books these days, even in those intended for young readers. Still, mass attitudes change slowly, especially among older people.

If parents want to foster their children's heterosexual development, they ought to begin with the basic understanding that homosexuality isn't completely separated from heterosexuality, as most of them believe. Even doctors often speak of someone as "a homosexual" instead of regarding him as a person who takes part in homosexual behavior. That may sound odd to you. If it does, consider the question of how much homosexual experience a person must have before he (or she) can be called "a homosexual." Is it one contact, or two, or a dozen, or an exclusive pattern?

About one out of every ten married men, according to Kinsey's *Sexual Behavior in the Human Male,* reported homosexual relations while they were still married. These men continued to have intercourse with their wives. Some were more homosexual than heterosexual, but others were the opposite.

Another popular belief is that a person who is aroused physically by a member of the same sex and suppresses that feeling is a "latent homosexual." Actually, this phrase can mean several different things. To some it means that homosexual desires are repressed—that is, they're not allowed to come into consciousness—but since they don't go away, they come into conflict with conscious heterosexuality. To others, the phrase means that if a person is aroused psychologically by someone of his own sex but doesn't have any actual physical contact, he's a latent homosexual.

The truth is that all of us are capable of doing every act imaginable. Under the proper circumstances, conditioning, and background, we could even murder someone, commit arson, or perform any kind of sexual act, illegal or not. You could say that we're all latent murderers, arsonists, or whatever. But that doesn't mean anything in terms of what we actually do. Similarly, all of us have latent homosexual tendencies to one degree or another, but that doesn't mean we're ever going to do anything about it.

It's a common experience to be stirred by a sexual feeling toward someone of the same sex through a fantasy, a dream, or in some other way. Most people are horrified by such thoughts and feel intensely guilty about having feelings they think are "perverted." Most of these people will never take part in a homosexual act, and the fleeting thoughts they have will never interfere with their heterosexual lives unless they carry guilt and fear into them.

Boys are the most intensely aware of the taboos against homosexuality during their adolescence. Taking histories from young boys, I've found that it's easier for them to tell me about their homosexual play before puberty than about their heterosexual experiences. That's because in those early years, homosexual contacts aren't considered taboo as they will be later. However, when these boys grow up to be adults, they find it easier to remember their heterosexual play before puberty, because by that time the taboos against homosexual behavior are greater than those against heterosexual activity.

If a boy thinks he's homosexually inclined and feels frightened, trapped, and even abandoned by society because of this, it won't do him any good to try to "give it all up." That isn't the way to stop being "a homosexual." Feelings are not easy to change or wish away.

Homosexuality is so much a fact of life today that parents would do better to admit it exists and talk about it with their children quietly, objectively, thoughtfully, and factually, instead of simply expressing hostility or resentment. It isn't going to go away, but it isn't increasing, and most boys don't grow up to be committed homosexuals at the "six" end of Kinsey's scale.

News accounts tell us constantly what a residue of hatred for the gay community there is in this country. "Fag," "fairy," and "queer" are still well-used words in the national vocabulary, and they are the words used when someone is beaten up on the street or in school because ignorant boys or men think he is gay. Most people still can't get themselves over the myth that you can always tell a gay person by the way he walks, or dresses, or behaves towards other men, or by other mannerisms. There *are* gays who can be identified this way, but as I said earlier, they are in the minority. Only about 15 percent of men with homosexual histories can be so identified, and there are males with one or more of these characteristics who aren't homosexual at all.

That's why parents rarely recognize it if their sons are homosexual. If they're concerned about such a possibility, they should take every opportunity they can to encourage and help their sons to develop heterosexuality, mostly by giving them maximum opportunities to have social contacts with girls. But if a son turns out to be gay, they should accept his sexual choice gracefully.

It seems to me sometimes that we actually promote homosexuality in younger boys by teasing them about their inexperienced attempts at going out with girls. Some parents keep such a close, rigid watch on these relationships that boys begin to feel there is something dirty, furtive, or secret about it. That kind of discouragement only puts a distance between children and their parents and accomplishes nothing. Similarly, if a boy is quiet, unathletic, interested in the arts but not in sports, worried parents should never push him to be another kind of person for fear he may be homosexual. Chances are he's just different, not interested in the same things most boys are, a state having nothing to do with his sexuality. That deadly word "sissy" should be avoided.

There's one fundamental fact both boys and their parents should remember. Only two sexes exist, and if a boy (or a girl) wants to have sexual relationships with another person and can't learn to develop the ability to do it with the opposite sex, he has only one alternative. That doesn't mean every man who fails to get married or doesn't go out with girls is certain to be homosexual, as so many people believe. But the way to homosexuality is much more open to such a man, and he may slip into that pattern of behavior simply because the other way isn't available.

Parents ought to play a dual role in a boy's life as he begins adolescence. They should encourage him to be interested in and to feel at ease with girls, and at the same time they should encourage him to be "one of the gang" where other boys are concerned.

No matter what your own feelings may be, you should be patient if you find that your parents aren't understanding or tolerant about homosexuality. Remember that even experts in the field are only beginning to understand the extremely complex behavioral pattern we call homosexuality. Anyone who says he has all the answers has to be taken with several tablespoons of salt. But we *do* know how important it is for parents to provide the warmth, love, and support their sons and daughters need as they make their adjustments to the world.

If a boy finds that his parents aren't able to give him as much of those qualities as he needs, he can help them by his own understanding and tolerance and by knowing it's only natural for them to worry about him and his sexuality. They want him to be happy and successful in every aspect of his life, including that one, and they have their own ideas of how he should achieve it, right or wrong. Those ideas usually translate into wanting him to live up to whatever code of conduct means a great deal to them.

I wouldn't want you to get the idea from reading what I've said here that if you have close friendships with other boys it implies any homosexuality in the relationship. Such friendships have always been an important part of growing up—look at Huck Finn and Tom Sawyer—and there may be nothing sexual whatever about them. You should never shy away from friendships because something you've heard or read makes you afraid homosexuality could be involved.

In fact, this country could use more of the warm, demonstrative friendships between men that are so characteristic of southern Europe and the Mediterranean countries, where males walk arm in arm or even with their arms around each other and no one thinks of them as homosexuals. Considering the way society is going, I very much doubt whether we'll ever get to that point in this country, but it certainly isn't wrong for men to show the same kind of affection toward each other that women do unselfconsciously. Our macho tradition is outdated.

It would be a good thing if we could shake off the old timidities, fears, and wrong ideas about male friendships. The "buddy" movies that have been so prevalent in the 1980s aren't the same thing; they simply show close friends sharing adventures together, not warm relationships. In a cold and threatening world, it isn't unreasonable to hope that men can learn to establish the same kind of rewarding relationships so common among women everywhere. Only tradition and the fear of being thought homosexual prevent it. We ought to banish that fear as though it were any other unreasonable dread. Does anyone really doubt that we'd live more healthy, fulfilled lives if we could?

CHAPTER · 10

"... I Forgot to Ask"

While reading this book, you may have thought of questions I haven't answered. I'm going to try now to anticipate what some of them might be and to provide the answers. You may not find your particular question here because there are so many thousands that could be asked. The questions that follow are real ones, some asked by sophomores, juniors, and seniors in a large eastern high school, others by junior high school students in the Chicago school system after lectures in their life-science classes. All the questions were asked anonymously.

> **1.** *Why is it that if girls sleep around, they're called sluts, but if boys do it, they come off as eligible bachelors, studs, or playboys?*

That's because of the double standard that has always prevailed. In your grandfather's time, people talked about a boy "sowing his wild oats," and it was winked at unless his conduct became scandalous and public. Girls were expected to be plaster saints. While that idea is not nearly as widely accepted today, as a result of the women's movement and changing times, the double standard is not dead, although it varies from one part of society to another and even from one region to another. But thankfully it seems to be slowly disappearing. Boys and girls should be equally responsible for what they do or don't do.

2. *Are necrophilia and bestiality moral or immoral?*

First, I'd better explain what they are, for those who might not know. Necrophilia is having sex with a dead person; bestiality is having sex with an animal. Necrophilia is considered immoral by nearly everyone, and it's also a crime. It is very rare sexual behavior. Bestiality, however, is a somewhat different matter. While most people think it's at least immoral, and repulsive as well, it's practiced around the world and has been known as far back as the ancient world. In our time, about 4 percent of city boys and 17 percent of farm boys, according to Kinsey's figures, engaged in sexual behavior with animals, and 4 percent of both city and farm girls had done it. As to whether it's immoral or not, that depends entirely on the point of view.

3. *What would happen if a boy had intercourse with an animal?*

Among boys who practice it, intercourse with animals is usually infrequent, but there are case histories of boys who build up a strong emotional attachment to a particular animal and have intercourse with it whenever possible. This behavior is against the law in every state. There are severe penalties for violations, and social ridicule accompanies discovery. Nevertheless, records of such cases can be found in our history from colonial days to the present.

While intercourse with animals is known technically as bestiality, it also comes under the broader heading of sodomy, which more commonly means both homosexual intercourse and anal intercourse with a woman.

This kind of sexual behavior may never happen to you, because the incidence is so low. If it does, you would be best advised to keep any knowledge of it to yourself so you can avoid either ridicule or punishment, or both. You can feel secure in your knowledge that you're not a monster, no matter what society may think about it.

4. *When is the fetus considered "human," and when is it no longer okay to have an abortion?*

Doctors, some of them, and other people don't agree on the first part of that question. Anti-abortion advocates think a fetus is "human" from the moment of conception. But in its landmark *Roe v. Wade* decision, the Supreme Court seemed to agree with most doctors by specifying three limitations on the right of states to regulate abortions. During the first trimester (three months) of pregnancy, it said, abortion "must be left to the judgment of the patient and the doctor." This, in effect, legalized abortion. But the court also ruled that for the second trimester, states could regulate "in ways that are reasonably related to maternal health," and for the third trimester, states were given the right to regulate or forbid abortion except where necessary "to preserve the life or health of the mother." In its 1989 decision discussed earlier, the court appeared to believe a fetus was viable at twenty weeks.

That last restriction was a confirmation of the belief of some doctors, namely, that in the second period the fetus is potentially capable of life outside the womb, and therefore this is when "life" begins. Doctors generally agree that the risks and problems mount considerably after the third month, while they are minimal in the first trimester.

5. *Is the size of the penis determined by any other part of the body?*

No. A tall, heavy man can have a short penis, and a short, slight man can have a large one. The average length is about six inches, but there is great variation. In any case, there's no connection between size and sexual ability.

6. *Can a girl get pregnant if there's sperm on a boy's hand and he puts his fingers into her vagina?*

Yes. It's not so likely to happen as if the penis were inside the vagina when ejaculation occurs, but if a boy masturbates, let's say, and his hand is covered with sperm and he immediately transfers it with his fingers to the vagina, pregnancy can result. I should repeat something I said earlier in the book, however: sperm cells that don't have the moist, warm vagina to live in, where they might be alive for hours, die quickly if they remain outside.

7. *What are the chances of getting AIDS from open-mouth kissing?*

No one has calculated the odds because not enough is known, and there is even some disagreement about whether this is possible. Some experts believe that the AIDS virus can be exchanged in saliva, but others think there might be a factor in saliva that *kills* AIDS.

8. *Are people weakened by having ejaculations?*

No way. On the contrary, the act often has a soothing effect, so that a person who is very tense may feel more relaxed after ejaculation. No matter how the orgasm is brought about, whether by masturbation, intercourse, or by some other method, what happens to the body is the same physiologically. Of course, society puts different values on these methods. For example, some people are upset by the idea of an aging man's getting an ejaculation through masturbation, although the same people don't care how often a younger, married man ejaculates when he has intercourse. Such attitudes are absurd and have nothing to do with reality. If a man's body should reach a physiological point where the amount of sex he has is more than he can handle, he won't be able to have an orgasm until he has rested for a while. The amount of time he'll need depends on his age, physical condition, and some psychological factors.

9. *Does a person have just so much sex to use up in his lifetime, and if a boy uses it up when he's young, will it prevent him from having a sex life when he's older?*

No, the body doesn't work that way. In fact, it seems to operate almost in the opposite fashion. Generally speaking, boys who start having sex the earliest —sex of some kind, that is—are the ones most likely to have the longest active sex lives and to have the most sex when they're older. That doesn't mean, however, that if a boy starts out deliberately to have a lot of sex when he's young he'll be guaranteed to have a lot when he's older. It means simply that bodies are different from each other. Some boys are more highly endowed with the ability to perform sexually throughout their lives.

10. *What is circumcision?*

There's a loose piece of skin extending to the end, or beyond the end, of the penis called a foreskin. In everyday medical practice, doctors once cut it off routinely a few days after a baby was born, but now most consider the procedure unnecessary. Removing this foreskin is called circumcision. It was done because it was believed easier to keep the head of the penis and the part just behind it cleaner if the skin was eliminated. All Jewish males are circumcised because that is part of their religion.

Sometimes the foreskin sticks to the head of the penis, and a circumcision is necessary to get it unstuck. Sometimes the foreskin has such a small opening that the head of the penis can't be pushed through. That's called phimosis. If a boy has that condition, it's possible to stretch the foreskin without circumcision. It can be done by inserting the tips of the forefinger of each hand into the opening of the foreskin and stretching it outward for about ten minutes every day. In two weeks or so, the skin will be stretched enough so the penis can emerge freely from it.

There's a white cheeselike substance called "smegma" that forms behind the head of the penis in uncircumcised men. It needs to be washed away every day because it has an unpleasant odor.

11. *What is "stone ache" or "lover's nuts"?*

It's the ache in the groin a boy gets when he's been fondling a girl for a long time, with an erection but no orgasm. It goes away after orgasm occurs, or if it doesn't happen, after a few hours. This condition is uncomfortable but not dangerous.

12. *What should I know about pubic hair?*

From your own observation, you know that it's the hair growing around the penis. It's also the hair that grows around a girl's sex organ. For some boys, as they grow older, a line of hair may grow up to the navel. A small number of girls also have this line.

A girl's pubic hair looks more triangular than a boy's, and it's usually the same color as her eyebrows. As people get older, pubic hair tends to go gray, just as hair on the head does, although it happens at a much slower rate. Pubic hair also grows from the scrotum (the bag holding your testicles), even in back of it and often around the anus. A girl's pubic hair doesn't interfere with intercourse because there isn't any on the inner lips of the vagina, or even on the inside of the outer lips.

13. *What is impotence?*

There are two kinds. The most common is erectile impotence, in which the male can't get an erection when he wants one. For a younger boy that can happen if he's frightened by something or is fearful he isn't going to get an erection.

Ejaculatory impotence is less common. That happens when a male can get an erection but can't ejaculate, when he wants to. The best way to overcome impotence of either kind is to accept it as a possibility and not feel you're no good if you can't perform. That will reduce anxiety, and chances are you'll then be able to get an erection and ejaculate.

14. *What is onanism?*

It's another word for masturbation. The word is taken from the story of Onan in the Bible (Genesis 38: 4–10), but to use this word is to misunderstand the story. Scholars now believe that when Onan "cast his seed upon the ground," the basis for the idea that he masturbated, he was actually having intercourse and then withdrew.

15. *What is the vulva?*

It's the female sex organ, and it consists of the opening to the vagina; the labia minora, which is the fold of skin just outside the opening; and the labia majora, the outer fold of skin enclosing the labia minora; it has hair growing on it.

16. *What is the vagina?*

The vagina is a tubelike structure, about three-and-one-half inches long. The penis enters it in intercourse, and it is very expandable—enough to accommodate the birth of a baby. The entire structure of the female sex organ, including the vulva and the vagina, are what is meant when they're commonly called "cunt" or "pussy."

17. *What is the clitoris?*

The clitoris is a small pealike structure at the top of the inner lips of the vagina, but enfolded by the outer lips. This organ is the female equivalent of the male penis, and as I've noted earlier, it's the focal point of stimulation in self-masturbation or stimulation by another person.

18. *Is there anything that will reduce the desire for sex, like saltpeter?*

For years there was a popular belief that saltpeter, a common drug, would inhibit sexual feelings. This powder was even put into coffee served in dormitories, prisons, or soldiers' and sailors' quarters. But the fact is that saltpeter has no effect whatever on human sexuality. Exhaustion and illness are the only two things that will really inhibit sex, although in men the massive injection of female hormones might do it.

19. *What happens when a girl menstruates?*

The process of menstruation is simply the sloughing off of the lining of the uterus once a month, about two weeks after the egg is passed down from the ovary through the uterus and into the vagina. During menstruation, the body is preparing for another egg to come down about two weeks in the future. Ordinarily, menstruation lasts from three to five days, but it may take as little as two days, or again as many as seven days or longer.

When she's menstruating, it may seem to the female that she's doing a lot of bleeding, but the actual amount passed is surprisingly small, mostly because menstrual blood is not like ordinary blood but is mixed with mucus.

During her menstrual period, the female wears a cotton menstrual pad called a "sanitary napkin" over her sex organ, or else she inserts a tubelike pad called a "tampon" to absorb the blood. During the period of heaviest flow, she may have to change pads three or four times a day. That usually occurs during the first days of her period.

Many girls feel embarrassed when they're menstruating. They used to be told to curtail activities like swimming or other sports, but few pay any attention to such ideas today and carry on their lives as usual. Some girls get cramps and headaches when they menstruate, and a boy may find that a girl acts a little differently during her period. But there's considerable variation. Some girls feel miserable; others take it in stride.

One of the things that might happen to a boy with a girl who's menstruating is to discover that she won't let him touch her sex organ even though he's done it before. There wouldn't be anything harmful about it if he did, and some people have intercourse right through a woman's menstrual period, even though it may be a little messy. There are also those of both sexes who won't have intercourse at this time for purely aesthetic reasons. This is particularly true of young boys and girls. Often it depends simply on how much two people are carried away by the sexual urge. It's also well to remember that the menstrual flow can transmit AIDS during oral sex.

While there are a good many familiar names for menstruation in the slang vocabulary, today most girls simply say they're having their period.

20. *What do girls like about sex?*

It would take another book to answer that question, and in fact, I've written such a book, called *Girls and Sex.* But I can give an answer here. As I've tried to show in some of the previous chapters, girls tend to be interested in the things that surround sex—that is, the time, the place, the mood—rather than in the specific physical aspects of the act itself.

When girls talk to other girls about boys and sex, they tend to speak more in generalities, of how "cute" the boy is, or how "nice." Sometimes, however, they may also talk about his build, or his good looks, or even the bulge in his crotch.

21. *Are there times when a girl either doesn't want or can't have intercourse?*

Of course there are times when a girl doesn't want intercourse, but the times vary from girl to girl. On the average, girls are more easily aroused for the day or two just before they menstruate and for the day or two following it. During menstruation is another time when they may feel especially sexual. However, this isn't true for all girls. Some don't seem to have these ups and downs in their sexual feelings. As I've said, there's no harm in having intercourse with a girl when she's menstruating, but a girl will probably not want to have it then if she has cramps, or if she thinks it's "messy," or because of social taboos stemming mostly from the Jewish faith, which characterizes menstruation as unclean.

In general, whether or not girls feel like having sex depends more on the mood they're in or the occasion. Many may not want to have sex when there's just been a quarrel, unless it's a part of "making up." Sometimes a place and time won't seem right to a girl, and then she doesn't want to have much, or any, sex play with a boy. Occasionally there may be a medical reason for a girl to avoid intercourse, or even fondling—for example, if she has an infection in her vagina or urethra.

22. *Do girls have as many orgasms as boys do in their teen years?*

As a rule, no. At fifteen, only a quarter of girls have had an orgasm from any source—or so the Kinsey figures showed. It's reasonable to believe, however, that this figure is much higher today. Yet by the same age, then and now, nearly 100 percent of the boys will have had orgasm at least once.

Of the girls who are having orgasms, the average has been from once in two weeks to three times in two weeks, but again, we have no reliable figures for the present, and presumably it could well be higher. In any case, most of the orgasms come from self-masturbation, just as they do with boys. A few girls, however, perhaps three in a hundred, have more orgasms than any boy, as girls are capable of five, ten, twenty, or even fifty orgasms one right after the other.

23. *Do particular foods stimulate the sex drive?*

No. The best way to do that is to get plenty of sleep, eat nourishing foods, and in general stay in good health. Don't believe those myths that foods like raw oysters, eggs, or malted milk will increase your sexual performance. They have no effect on it at all. If a boy is in good health, he'll most likely be able to perform sexually as close to his capacity as possible.

24. *What is Spanish fly?*

It's a powdered drug called "cantharides" that irritates the lining of the urethra. Spanish fly is popularly believed to make a female very excited sexually, but there's no truth in this idea. Moreover, if it's taken in large enough quantities, it can be highly poisonous. In fact, now that we're on the subject, there is no such thing as a drug or any other kind of stimulant that will make either females or males sexually excited—what is known as an aphrodisiac, after the goddess of love,

Aphrodite. Nevertheless, people have always been looking for such a potion, and even today the rhinoceros is facing extinction because so many people believe that powder ground from its horn is an aphrodisiac. There is, let me repeat, no such thing.

25. *What should I know about prostitutes?*

A prostitute is a girl or woman who has sex for money. Slang terms for prostitute include "hustler," "streetwalker," and "call girl." Teen-agers today are careless about words, though, and sometimes they use the word "slut" to mean a prostitute, which may not be the case. A slut may be no more than a promiscuous woman.

Prostitutes themselves refer to their work as being "in the life." This "life" ranges from those who walk the streets or stand on curbs and solicit men who pass by walking or in cars, all the way through different stages of apartment "life" to the high-priced call girl who may get a four-figure payment from a rich client for a night, or part of one. Prostitution is more of a class-conscious occupation in this country now than it ever was. The lowest class of prostitutes cluster around construction sites, for example, and the highest class are part of the corporate entertainment structure.

Boys who might contemplate beginning their sexual experience with girls by finding a prostitute should think several times about it. For one thing, the experience itself is likely to be unsatisfying, since no love or affection is involved, the prostitute is usually in a hurry, and she responds sexually not at all unless she fakes it. Secondly, there is great danger of venereal disease, particularly AIDS, because there is no way of knowing if any of her recent sexual partners have been infected. The high-priced call girl may be a somewhat different matter, but young boys are not likely to be in that market.

You know the word "pimp," I'm sure, and probably know what it means, but perhaps you don't know that this man who manages a prostitute and takes most or all of her money is also likely to have sex with her, thus multiplying the risk of disease transmission. We use the word pimp in a broader way, too, for someone who gets something illegally for someone else, or as a general term of contempt for a man who is weak, shifty, or otherwise worthless.

26. *What about male prostitutes?*

This is a more highly organized business than it used to be, and is common all over the world. Since male semen can transmit HIV, the chance of acquiring AIDS is also increased, although infected needles from drug users is now the most common kind of transmission. Unlike the relationship with a female prostitute, where the customer ejaculates, in male prostitution, the customer, in most cases, pays for the privilege of having the prostitute ejaculate. There are also male prostitutes, much fewer in number, who are paid by women.

27. *What is a hermaphrodite?*

A true hermaphrodite is a person who has the gonads of both sexes—that is, testicles and ovaries. There are very few of these people in existence. However, there are pseudohermaphrodites, who are in between the two sexes—a boy, perhaps, with a tiny penis, like a clitoris, or a girl with a large clitoris, almost like a penis. Very often corrective surgery or hormone therapy can be given to make these people more like a male or female.

The word is sometimes also applied to others, such as men with large breasts, like women's, or a woman with no breasts at all, or a woman with hair on her face, like a man. These people are not really hermaphrodites, and their problem is usually the result of some disturbance in their hormone balance. The coined words "amorphadite" or "morphadite" are often mistakenly used for the correct word.

28. *What is castration?*

Castration is the removal of the gonads. The gonads are the main source of hormones, so that when a prepubescent or adolescent boy is castrated, there is no growth of hair on the face, the rest of the hair on his body becomes fine and silky, his voice remains high, he cannot ejaculate, and often he can't get an erection. The word for such a person is "eunuch," (pronounced *yew-nuk*). However, if he's castrated as an older man, there will be less effect, in proportion to his age. Girls can also be castrated by having their ovaries removed. In some countries there is also the barbaric custom of clitoris circumcision as a tribal rite. Disease, especially cancer, is the only reason for male castration these days.

29. *What is abnormal sex?*

This question can't really be answered, and let me explain why. The word "abnormal" has several meanings as far as sex is concerned. For instance, it can mean something that's unusual or rare. By that definition, it would be abnormal to have intercourse while you were eating and drinking at the same time. On the other hand, masturbation is normal because nearly all boys do it. Even homosexuality would be almost normal by this definition since so large a percentage of boys have experienced such behavior at least once.

But we can also look at what is abnormal by thinking of what's unnatural. We're all mammals, and so our sexual behavior, which is like that of other mammals, is natural. Other mammals of the nonhuman kind engage in nearly every kind of sexual activity that we do. So from that standpoint there's really nothing humans do sexually that's abnormal.

There's a third way to look at it, however—the way our own society considers sexual behavior. Our laws and churches have laid down rules about it, although they don't always agree. For example, it isn't against the law to masturbate. It's the most common of human sexual activities. But even in this era of acceptance we

live in, there are still religious leaders and their followers, as well as other people with rigid moral ideas, who
think it's not only wrong but abnormal. It *is* against the
law in most states to put your mouth on the sex organ
of another person, but oddly enough there are some
religious people who don't think that's wrong. According to the law, by and large, most of our sexual
behavior outside marriage is considered wrong, and
religious organizations mostly agree.

Still another way to consider what may be abnormal is to look at what sexual acts do harm to other
people. I mean things like forcing other people to
engage in sexual behavior against their will, or to lie or
cheat or seduce them into doing what they don't want
to do. These acts would be considered abnormal by
most of us.

So you can see what a complicated business it is
trying to decide what's abnormal sex and what isn't.
That's why I said the question couldn't be answered
easily and quickly, or at all. What people think is "abnormal" in sex is determined very much by what they
think of as "normal," and it hasn't much to do with the
actual behavior of people in general.

30. *What is a wet dream?*

A boy may wake up at night, or in the morning, to
find he's had an ejaculation while he was asleep. That
may be puzzling, even frightening, to boys who've
heard it said that the loss of semen in sleep is somehow
damaging. Actually, it's no more damaging than the

loss of it in masturbation or intercourse. It's simply the result of sexual excitement, usually through dreaming, which eventually reaches the point of climax with the emission of semen. It isn't an automatic substitute for intercourse, or a means of relieving sexual tension. In fact, it may often come soon after a sex experience.

31. *What can you do about erections if you get them in a public place?*

The best thing is to try to think of other, nonsexual things. If you can, your penis will become soft again. Or you can put your fingers in your pockets in such a way that the effect will be minimized by pushing your jeans or trousers out a little. Another way would be to wear a sweater or a jacket that comes down far enough —but then, of course, you'd have to anticipate what was going to happen, and that's not likely. Some boys wear an athletic supporter—the common jockstrap, in other words—which will hold down the penis. Boys ordinarily wear these in games to give the penis and testicles protection and support. Aside from all these possible remedies, however, there isn't much you can do if you happen to be wearing tight blue jeans. In that case, you can't very well hide what's there.

32. *What is adultery, and what is fornication?*

Maybe you thought they were the same thing. Not true. Adultery is sexual intercourse when one or both persons are married, but not to each other. This is the legal definition. Fornication, again in legal terms, is intercourse when neither partner is married. In all the states, adultery is against the law, and in about half of them, fornication is illegal. You can see now what I meant earlier in the book when I said that if our sex laws were strictly enforced, more people would be in jail than out.

33. *What is sadomasochism?*

This is a contraction of two words, "sadism" and "masochism." Sadism is the receiving of sexual pleasure from giving pain to someone else. Masochism is the receiving of sexual pleasure from pain inflicted by someone else. In both cases, the consent of each party is necessary. The two words are contracted into one because in most cases people who get some sexual pleasure from hurting others also usually get it from being hurt.

Sadism and masochism can also be used in a non-sexual sense. If a person is a bully who enjoys beating up on other people but gets no sexual pleasure from it, we can truthfully say he's sadistic. If someone enjoys being humiliated even when the incident is not connected with sex, he (or she) may be called a masochist. This is common usage, but these terms are often used incorrectly.

There's some sadomasochism in most of us. When people become aroused sexually, they often enjoy nibbling, biting, and scratching when they're doing these things, and also when it's being done to them. But there are others who, for reasons not entirely clear, develop much stronger sadomasochistic behavior. They enjoy being spanked or beaten, whipped, humiliated, tied down, or something similar. Or they may enjoy doing these things to someone else. It isn't uncommon for boys to fantasize or think of such activity when they masturbate or at other times. It's only when some of these fantasies are put into practice that there's cause to worry.

34. *What is incest?*

From a legal standpoint, incest is having sexual intercourse with a relative of the opposite sex. The relative could be a mother, father, brother, sister, grandparent, or grandchild, and in some states, uncles or aunts or first cousins. Usually it also includes stepparents, stepchildren, and stepbrothers and sisters, even though they are not blood relatives. The same is true for adopted children.

In a broader sense, incest doesn't have to mean sexual intercourse but includes any kind of sexual relations, including homosexual ones, between relatives. However, sex play with sisters and brothers and cousins is not at all unusual in a preadolescent boy or girl.

The taboo against incest is the oldest sexual taboo of all—it goes back to the earliest times—and it's also the strongest. Guilt alone is a strong inhibition, and of course all religions absolutely forbid it. Medical reasons have also been cited for the taboo. Until recently scientists believed that children of an incestuous union would be likely to inherit the worst weaknesses, mental or physical, on both sides of the family, even though they would be just as likely to inherit the outstanding good characteristics of both. It was argued that genetically speaking, continuing incestuous relationships in a group would tend to "breed out"—that is, the bad traits would eventually overcome the good ones in successive generations. These long-held beliefs have been attacked by recent research, and serious doubts have been raised about their validity.

35. *Is it possible to get pregnant without having intercourse?*

It's possible but it doesn't happen very often. Sperm are like tadpoles that move forward under their own power, and if a boy ejaculates near the opening of the vagina, even if his penis doesn't enter at all, it's possible for the sperm to work themselves along the entire length of the vagina and up into the uterus.

36. *Should children be allowed to run around the house without any clothes on?*

We're often told about how beautiful the human body is and how wrong it is to be ashamed of it, but if that's true, then why are so many people ashamed to show their naked bodies in front of other people? The answer is that we still live in a society that hasn't given up on the Puritanism we began with, and we have to accept that fact. People can't be as free as they might like to be because others will be offended. In the privacy of your own home, however, it's possible to be relaxed about nudity, if the at-home standards are different from those of society. Parents are the ones who set these standards, and they're the ones who will determine, to a large extent, how much nudity will be tolerated and where and when. It remains true, no matter what standards are applied, that the human body is beautiful, and we should feel no shame in viewing it.

37. *What's the difference between sex and love?*

They're really separate things. It's possible to have a great deal of affection for parents, your dog, or your best friend without having sex enter the picture. It's also possible to have sex with other people in a hostile, even cruel way without having any affection for them. In most cases, though, love to some degree and sexual feelings are part of the same response to someone else. When these two things occur together, it can be one of the most profound and meaningful experiences it's possible to have.

My own belief is that being "in love" is not something separate and distinct from being "not in love" but is part of a scale—say, from zero to a hundred. If you have a girl friend you like, you're somewhere along the lower end of the scale. But as you get to know her better, take her out more, and like her even more, you move up the scale until you experience butterflies in the stomach when you see her, find yourself thinking of her constantly, and so you can say positively, "I'm in love." But you may still be a long way from the top of the scale, and as you continue going out with her, you'll find your position probably changes in one direction or the other on the scale.

It works out better if affection is the beginning of the relationship, with sexual feelings entering the picture later, rather than the other way around. Infatuation, or puppy love, often comes very quickly. Sometimes it happens the first time you see a girl, but it takes a long time, if ever, for that to develop into the kind of love that's based on trust, understanding, consideration, and open communication.

38. *What is a nymphomaniac?*

It was once believed that some women had insatiable sexual appetites and could never be satisfied. The same condition in men was called "satyriasis." Dr. Kinsey exploded this idea in his reports on sexuality in the human male and female by showing that there was the widest possible variation in human sexual activity and there was nothing that could be considered "too much" or "too little." Kinsey himself defined a nymphomaniac as "someone who has more sex than you do."

Afterword

I'd like to say something about sex in relation to the remainder of a boy's life, since it doesn't exist as something separate and apart from day-to-day living. Sex is very important, true, but its importance shouldn't be overemphasized. Even in adolescence, when a boy is nearing the peak of his sexuality, the amount of time he spends in having some kind of sexual activity or in thinking about it doesn't constitute more than a small part of a total day.

If a boy masturbates, for example, it may take two or twenty minutes out of the day or night. If he goes out with a girl, the sexual part of the occasion, if any, may take up only an hour or so, and he surely won't be doing this every day of the week. Younger boys may get an erection up to seven or more times a day, but it doesn't last long, and as these boys get older, the frequency decreases. A boy may have sexual dreams at night, but again, he may have other kinds of dreams, too, and many of them aren't even remembered.

Clearly sex is an important part of our lives, but it's a rather small part of anyone's total existence, as far as actual time is concerned. When boys spend a good part of their waking days thinking about sex, or doing something sexual, it's usually because they're upset about it—feeling guilty about it, or anxious, or unsure. I hope this book will relieve boys of some of those guilt feelings, anxieties, and uncertainties. If it does, it's certain to decrease the amount of time they spend thinking about or actively engaging in sex.

If that sounds to you as though I'm suggesting you shouldn't become too involved with sex, my answer is that sex is worthwhile and pleasurable, but if you feel guilty or anxious about it, something valuable is lost. That something is what makes you feel an inch small or ten feet high.

One important thing to remember. It isn't what you do sexually that matters, *as long as you're not hurting someone else.* It's how you feel about what you're doing that counts. If a boy learns nothing more from these pages, that fact alone can make the difference between leading a whole life and leading only part of one.

As a boy grows up, he finds that society is sometimes restrictive about what it allows him to do sexually, or at least it tries to be. But on the other hand, he's constantly stimulated by everything around him —movies, television, advertisements, what girls wear, magazines, and the behavior of some girls. In short, he finds himself in a society that seems to be preoccupied with sex yet imposes prohibitions on his behavior. He may violate these prohibitions every day in the week, but they don't go away.

I know this is going to sound more than a little old-fashioned, but you'll be surprised to know that your great-grandfather knew something about this situation, too. He often heard a rhyme, almost forgotten now, but once familiar to nearly everyone in the country:

> Mother, may I go out to swim?
> Yes, my darling daughter;
> Hang your clothes on a hickory limb,
> And don't go near the water.

It's my hope that this book will teach boys how to swim without drowning in a social sea that may not be as angry and restrictive as it was in grandfather's day, but because of its unprecedented freedom and acceptance may be twice as confusing.

For Further Reading

Arnold, Caroline. *Sex Hormones: Why Males and Females Are Different.* New York: Morrow, 1981.

Bell, Ruth, et al. *Changing Bodies, Changing Lives: A Book for Teens on Sex and Relationships.* New York: Random House, 1981.

Eagan, Andrea B. *Why Am I So Miserable if These Are the Best Years of My Life?* New York: Harper & Row, 1976.

Hamilton, Eleanor. *Sex, with Love: A Guide for Young People.* Boston: Beacon Press, 1978.

Hein, Karen, and Theresa Foy DiGeronimo. *AIDS: Trading Fears for Facts.* New York: Consumer Reports Books, 1989.

Hettlinger, Richard. *Growing Up with Sex: A Guide for the Early Teens,* rev. ed. New York: Continuum, 1980.

Hopper, C. Edmund, and William A. Allen. *Sex Education for Physically Handicapped Youth.* Springfield, IL: C.C. Thomas, 1980.

Johnson, Eric. *Love and Sex in Plain Language,* 3rd ed. New York: Harper & Row, 1985.

Lena, Dan, and Marie Howard. *Hands Off . . . I'm Special! How to Tell Your Boyfriend No.* Hollywood, FL: Compact Books, 1987.

McGuire, Paula. *It Won't Happen to Me: Teenagers Talk About Pregnancy.* New York: Delacorte Press, 1983.

Madaras, Lynda. *Lynda Madaras Talks to Teens About AIDS: An Essential Guide for Parents, Teachers, and Young People.* New York: Newmarket Press, 1988.

Marsh, Carole. *I Con . . . If You Con(dom): The Ins and Outs of Contraception for the Sexually Active Girl or Boy.* Bath, NC: Gallopade Publishing Group, 1987.

————*Sex Stuff for Boys: Sperm, Squirm, and Other Squiggly Stuff.* Bath, NC: Gallopade Publishing Group, 1987.

————*Sex Stuff for Girls: A Period Is More Than a Punctuation Mark.* Bath, NC: Gallopade Publishing Group, 1987.

————*STD Is Not Motor Oil: The Truth and Consequences of Sexually Transmitted Diseases.* Bath, NC: Gallopade Publishing Group, 1987.

Sciacca, Fran, and Jill Sciacca. *Sex: When to Say Yes.* Don Mills, ON, Canada: Worldwide, 1987.

Voss, Jacqueline, and Jay Gale. *A Young Woman's*

Guide to Sex. Los Angeles: Price Stern Sloan, 1988.

Westheimer, Ruth, and Nathan Kravetz. *First Love: A Young People's Guide to Sexual Information.* New York: Warner Books, 1987.

Wood, Barry. *Questions Teenagers Ask About Dating and Sex.* Old Tappan, NJ: Revell, 1981.

Index

About the Author

WARDELL B. POMEROY received the A.B. degree and M.A. degree in psychology from Indiana University, and the Ph.D. degree from Columbia University. As research associate at the Institute for Sex Research, he was co-author with the late Alfred Kinsey of *Sexual Behavior in the Human Male* and *Sexual Behavior in the Human Female*. He is academic dean emeritus at the Institute for Advanced Study of Human Sexuality in San Francisco, where he lives with his family.